Topos. European Landscape Magazine (Ed.)
Topos. Europäisches Magazin für Landschaftsarchitektur (Hrsg.)

Stucco, Stone and Steel
Stuck, Stein und Stahl

New Materials in Open Space Design
Neue Materialien für den öffentlichen Raum

Callwey Verlag, München

Birkhäuser – Publishers for Architecture / Verlag für Architektur
Basel · Boston · Berlin

Topos
EUROPEAN
LANDSCAPE
MAGAZINE

Cover: Heike Ossenkop
Cover-Photos: Kamel Louafi,
Giordano Tironi, Alan Ward

NICOLE UHRIG **6**
Landschaft en vogue
Landscape en vogue

STEFANO BOERI **15**
*Neapel: Materialtest für den
Städtebau*
Naples: Makeshift materials
as urban development
strategy

MARTIN REIN-CANO **27**
LORENZ DEXLER
Berlin: Grafik auf Asphalt
Berlin: Drawing on asphalt

Graphics on asphalt in the courtyard of a Berlin firm. Page 27

JONAS BERGLUND **37**
*Jordbro: Kiefern im Corten-
Stahl-Rahmen*
Jordbro: Pine trees within a
Cor-Ten steel surround

ALFRED BERGER **40**
TIINA PARKKINEN
*Berlin: die Botschaften der
nordischen Länder*
Berlin: The Nordic embassy
complex

A wooden platform and magnolias show employees to the garden of an insurance company in Tilburg. Page 12

ADRIAAN GEUZE **12**
*Tilburg: Magnolien im
Schieferbeet*
Tilburg: Magnolias in a bed
of slate

STEFAN ROTZLER **18**
MATTHIAS KREBS
*Basel: Feigenernte an der
Schönaustraße*
Basel: A harvest of figs at
Schönaustrasse

CARME PINOS **30**
*Torrevieja: Holz für die
Felsenküste*
Torrevieja: Wood for a rocky
coast

GIORDANO TIRONI **22**
Genf: Erinnerung in Stein
Geneva: Memories in Stone

THORBJÖRN **33**
ANDERSSON
*Stockholm: Recycling von
Natur und Geschichte*
Stockholm: Re-using nature
and history

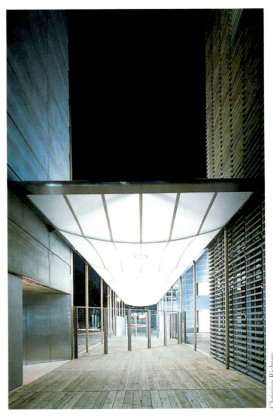

Light makes the fabric canopy suspended over the entrance to the
Nordic countries' embassies seem weightless. Page 40

Concrete thresholds lend dynamics to the garden of the water crater in Bad Oeynhausen. Page 62

MARTHA SCHWARTZ **45**
SHAUNA
GILLIES-SMITH
*Manchester: »Pudding-Stein«
trifft Granit und Stahl*
Manchester: "Pudding-
stone" meets granite and steel

WALTER VETSCH **49**
Lust auf Details
A fancy for details

BERNARD LASSUS **54**
*Schein und Wirklichkeit des
Materials*
Appearance and reality of
the material

HENRI BAVA **62**
*Magisches Wasser in
Ostwestfalen*
Magical water in Westphalia

CHRIST-JAN **72**
VAN ROOIJ
MARTIN KNUIJT
*Zutphen: Atmosphäre
schaffen durch Kontraste*
Zutphen: Creating an at-
mosphere through contrasts

JOHANNA GIBBONS **76**
*London: Backstein und Farb-
flächen*
London: Bricks and
coloured surfaces

BENGT ISLING **80**
Schweden: die Farbe Grau
Sweden: The colour grey

PHILIPP SATTLER **89**
Wenig, das aber richtig
A little means a lot

MARIA AUBÖCK **96**
JANOS KARASZ
*Public Design: Das Vertraute
modulieren*
Public design: Modulating
the familiar

Oiled lime stucco at the Expo in Hannover. Page 65

BERND KRÜGER **57**
*Produktentwicklung mit
Aluminium*
Production development
with aluminium

STEFAN LEPPERT **65**
*Hannover: Gärten der
Materialvielfalt*
Hannover: Gardens of mate-
rial diversity

BART BRANDS **84**
KAREL LOEFF
*Holland: Hardware versus
Software*
Holland: Hardware versus
software

Strips of lavender and crushed stone are edged in metal on the grounds of a factory in Saxony. Page 89

Editorial   **4/5**
Authors   **100**
Photo Credits/   **102**
Translations
Impressum   **104**

*M*atter, that troublesome mass that never wants to do what we want. That awkward material that resists the designer, won't stand up to gravity, blows budgets and is wreaked by the users. In fact, the enemy of all great minds venturing into the lower depths of applied physics. There is so much to keep in mind: dimensional stability, shearing strain, moisture expansion, thermal shrinkage, transverse contraction constant, Euro per square metre and resistance to wear with inexpert installation. And yet the term is so simply and aptly defined: "substance that can be experienced with the senses, occupies space and forms the basis of physical bodies." Senses? Bodies?

Anyone kissed by the muses will perk up. Doesn't a proper kiss involve senses and bodies? Matter instantly turns into passion, material into the incarnation of feelings. Profane technical aspects of construction must recede behind noble artistic ones in order for a pile of sand, structural steel and tarpaper to become animated by the genius of the architectural artist.

There are many materials and just as many reasons for using one or the other: concrete suits a rocky landscape, metal recalls earlier industrial uses, wood warms people's bottoms. Universally valid rules dictating which material is right and proper and socially acceptable for what place hardly exist any longer. Most taboos have made way for the 'anything goes' of western liberalism. Everything that was not up to snuff yesterday can already be smart tomorrow – remember the meteoric rise of Cor-Ten steel. Sculptors such as Richard Serra heaved it up from heavy industry into the higher spheres of fine art. Then, after years of effort at familiarisation, it was demoted back to architecture and eventually even became respectable for public spaces. Trailblazing is over. It is only in countries with moral depth, such as Germany, that the use of tropical wood (which destroys the rainforest), chemically polluted railway ties and atomic energy-produced aluminium continues to be condemned. But otherwise?

The paradise of 'liberté, egalité, materialité' is open to everyone who is not afraid of the hell of arbitrariness. "It's all so nice and colourful here, I just can't decide," shrieked the German pop star Nina Hagen in the 80s. Architectural clients feel much the same way; it is up to the designer to decide. He faces no arguments in an age when all is technically doable and aesthetic authorities are non-existent.

When in doubt, respecting the economic clout of his client, the designer hands over some nice figures to assist in the decision-making on the choice of materials dictated by his will to form. Matter needs ideas.

Materie, das ist die lästige Masse, die nie so will wie man selbst. Das sperrige Material, das sich dem Entwerfer widersetzt, der Schwerkraft nicht standhält, Kostenrahmen sprengt und von Nutzern zerstört wird. Eigentlich der Feind aller Geistesgrößen, die sich in die Niederungen der angewandten Physik begeben. An was man nicht alles denken muss: Werkstofffestigkeit, Schubverformung, Feuchtigkeitsausdehnung, Wärmeschrumpfung, Querkontraktionskonstante, Euro pro Quadratmeter und Verschleißfestigkeit beim Einbau durch Dilettanten. Dabei lässt sich der Begriff so treffend einfach definieren: Materie ist »Raum einnehmender, durch die Sinne erfahrbarer Stoff, der die Grundlage physikalischer Körper bildet«. Sinne, Körper? Da wachen die von der Muse Geküssten auf. Gehören zu jedem anständigen Kuss nicht Sinne und Körper? Und schon wird die Materie zur Leidenschaft, Material zur Inkarnation von Gefühl. Die profanen technischen Seiten des Bauens müssen zurücktreten hinter den noblen künstlerischen, damit ein Haufen Sand, Baustahl und Teerpappe vom Genius des Baukünstlers belebt werde.

Materialien gibt es viele, und ebenso viele Gründe, das eine oder das andere einzusetzen: Beton passt in die Felslandschaft, Metall erinnert an frühere industrielle Nutzung, Holz hält den Hintern warm. Allgemeingültige Regeln dafür, welches Material an welchem Ort recht, billig und gesellschaftlich genehm ist, existieren kaum mehr, die meisten Tabus sind dem »anything goes« des westlichen Liberalismus gewichen. Alles was gestern pfui war, kann morgen schon hui sein – man denke an den kometenhaften Aufstieg des Corten-Stahls, den Bildhauer wie Richard Serra aus der Schwerindustrie in die höheren Sphären der Kunst hievten, bevor er in jahrelanger Gewöhnungsarbeit wieder in die Architektur hinab dekliniert und schließlich auch im öffentlichen Raum salonfähig wurde. Die Pionierarbeit ist vollbracht. Nur in Ländern mit moralischem Tiefgang wie Deutschland werden regenwaldvernichtendes Tropenholz, chemieverseuchte Bahnschwellen und Atomstrom-Aluminium weiterhin verflucht. Aber sonst?

Das Paradies der »liberté, egalité, materialité« steht allen offen, die sich nicht vor der Hölle der Willkür fürchten. »Es ist alles so schön bunt hier, ich kann mich gar nicht entscheiden«, kreischte Nina Hagen in den 80ern. Den Bauherren geht's ähnlich, entscheiden muss der Gestalter. Argumente hat er keine im Zeitalter der technischen Machbarkeit und der fehlenden ästhetischen Instanzen. Im Zweifelsfall reicht er dem wirtschaftlichen Primat seines Auftraggebers gehorchend schöne Zahlen als Entscheidungshilfe für die Auswahl der Materialien, die ihm sein Formwille diktiert. Materie braucht Ideen.

Lisa Diedrich

Landschaft en vogue

Landscape en vogue

Nicole Uhrig

»Frauen und Möbel verändern sich in der Regel gleichzeitig«, schrieb Jacques Laurent, ein Zeitgenosse des ausgehenden 19. Jahrhunderts über die verblüffende Ähnlichkeit der Damenmode und des Möbeldesigns. Allzusehr dürfte uns diese Beobachtung nicht überraschen. Ist doch die Mode ebenso Ausdruck von Kultur und Gesellschaft wie Musik, Literatur, Design und Architektur. Darf man die Landschaftsarchitektur hinzufügen? Natürlich, jedenfalls solange sich die Diskussion um kunsthistorische Stilrichtungen und Epochen dreht. Wer es jedoch wagt, Landschaftsarchitektur als modisch oder trend-orientiert zu bezeichnen, der beleidigt so manch überzeugten Gestalter. Es ist aber nicht von der Hand zu weisen, dass Planer auch gewissen Trends huldigen. Natürlich bekennt sich niemand zur Auswahl eines Materials, weil es derzeit „in" ist. Das gilt als unehrenhaft, denn das Berufsethos verlangt nach konzeptionellen Argumenten.

Zusehends befördern die Medien Superstars der Architektur- und Landschaftsarchitektur nach oben, und mit ihnen auch Starprojekte, die als Inspirationsquellen tatsächlich gute Dienste leisten. Ein ausgewähltes Sortiment von Image-Bildern findet sich in Wettbewerbsbeiträgen und Veröffentlichungen wieder. Solche qualitativ hochwertigen, digital optimierten Projektfotos transportieren aber mehr atmosphärische Ästhetik als Information. Sie lassen sich stilistisch von professioneller Produktwerbung genauso wenig unterscheiden wie von der Modefotografie. Und der Betrachter bleibt gewöhnlich mit der Frage zurück: »Wie sieht der Anzug – und vor allem das Model – denn nun wirklich aus?« Ähnliche Zweifel wirft die stimmungsvolle Fotografie einer Sitzbank im Grünen auf.

Die Geschwindigkeit, mit der sich Stilrichtungen, Trends und Moden durchsetzen, sind indes abhängig vom Adressaten. Vom Vorsprung der Modebranche einmal abgesehen, war die Landschaftsarchitektur immer etwas langsamer als die Architektur. So bescherte die Mode uns schon in den 80er Jahren Krawatten in Kandinsky-Optik, violette Blazer mit Schultern wie Sofakissen und mintfarbene Barhocker auf Konfettimuster-Böden. Erst in den 90er Jahren standen in den Straßen unserer Städte Laternen, Papierkörbe und Sitzbänke in Serienfarbe Erika, und die Spielplätze protzten mit zackig geformten, blassgrünen Gummi-Wiesen und lila Wackeltierchen. Ebenso fanden die Ausdrucksformen der Graffiti- und Breakdance-

Über Trends rümpfen Planer meist die Nase, doch sie bringen die Profession voran – mit neuen Materialien, Formen und Farben.

While trends usually make planners turn up their noses, they do cause the profession to advance – with new materials, forms and colours.

"As a rule, women and furniture change at the same time." This statement by Jacques Laurent, who lived at the end of the 19th century, refers to the astonishing similarities between womens' fashions and furniture design. We should not find this observation all that surprising, seeing as how fashion is as much an expression of culture as music, literature, design and architecture. Are we allowed to mention landscape architecture in this context? Of course, that is, as long as the discussion is limited to art historical styles and eras. Yet anyone who dares to call landscape architecture fashionable or trend-oriented will offend many a dedicated designer. Nevertheless, it cannot be denied that planners also make decisions according to fashionable criteria. Of course no one would admit choosing a particular kind of material because it is trendy. This would be considered dishonourable, for professional ethics demand that the argument be conceptual.

The media visibly promote superstars in architecture and landscape architecture and with them the star projects actually serving a good purpose as sources of inspiration. A selection of pictures projecting a certain image can be found over and over again in competition entries and publications. Such high-quality digitally optimised project photos, however, convey more atmosphere and aesthetics than information. They are no different in style from product advertising or fashion photography. And they usually leave the viewer asking: "What does this suit, and especially this model, really look like?" Similar doubts arise with a photo full of atmosphere of a bench surrounded by greenery. The speed at which styles, trends and fashions assert themselves depends, in turn, on their audience. Apart

Was dem Skater seine Hose mit Bundweite nicht unter 40, das ist dem Landschaftsarchitekten seine Wandverkleidung aus poliertem Edelstahl. Kleider verraten uns genauso viel über Kultur und Gesellschaft wie Musik, Literatur, Design, Architektur und Landschaftsarchitektur. Alle unterliegen Moden – und zeigen die Lust, in der eigenen Zeit zu leben.

What trousers with a waist size not under 40 are to a skater, cladding of polished high-grade steel is to the landscape architect. Clothes tell us just as much about civilisation and society as music, literature, design, architecture and landscape architecture. They are all subject to and promote fashion – and demonstrate the desire to live in one's own time.

Szene erst viel später ihren Weg in die Freiraumplanung. Die Gestalter verzierten die Mauern ihrer Parks mit eigens entworfenen Graffiti oder formten gleich die gesamte Mauer als abstrahierten Schriftzug. Vom einst rebellischen Charakter des Graffiti blieb freilich nicht viel übrig. Dass die Architektur der Landschaftsarchitektur eine Nasenlänge voraus war, zeigen

die nackten Sichtbetonmauern und der rostige Corten-Stahl, die im Außenraum salonfähig wurden, als sie in der Architektur längst zum Standard gehörten. Aber die Landschaftsarchitektur holt auf: Zu unserer Freude greifen Architekten nun in die Materialkiste der Freiraumgestalter – so versahen die Schweizer Jacques Herzog und Pierre de Meuron ihren hinlänglich publizierten kalifornischen Weinkeller mit einer Fassade ganz aus Gabionen, bisher ein typisches Freiraum-Material.

from the avant-garde nature of the fashion industry, landscape architecture was always somewhat slower than architecture. Thus fashion in the 80s presented us with ties decorated with Kandinsky prints, purple blazers with shoulders like sofa cushions, and mint-coloured bar stools on confetti print linoleum. It was not until the 90s that our streets sported lanterns, rubbish bins and benches in the serially produced tint of heather, and playgrounds flaunted zigzag shaped, pale green rubber meadows and purple wobbly animals. Similarly, the graffiti and breakdance scene's forms of expression only made their way into open space planning with a considerable time lag. Designers then decorated walls in their parks with specially designed graffiti or gave a whole wall the shape of an abstract text to begin with. Not much of the original rebellious nature of graffiti was left, of course. Architecture's position ahead of landscape architecture by a nose is illustrated by the bare, exposed concrete walls and rusty Cor-Ten steel that only became acceptable in outdoor spaces long after they had become standard in architecture. But landscape architecture is catching up: we are delighted that architects have now picked up ideas from the green profession: for instance, Herzog & de Meuron in the gabion-like facade of their adequately published Californian winery.

Current trends are taken up more and more quickly from one day to the next. In the lead is the department store Hennes+Mauritz, that replaces its complete collection every six weeks. Colour and elaborate forms were withdrawn in all lines at the beginning of the 90s. In fashion everything unnecessary was radically cut. There were zippers and covered rows of fasteners instead

Nach den fetten 80er Jahren mit ihrer Farbskala von Mintgrün bis Violett trat in den 90ern Ausgeflipptes in den Hintergrund. Strenge Linien und rohe Materialien prägen viele Bauten und Freiräume. In der Berliner Großsiedlung Marzahn nehmen Heike Langenbach und Roman Ivancsics mit ihrer Gestaltung des Barnimplatzes die einfache Geometrie der Plattenbauten auf.

After the fat 80s with colours ranging from mint green to violet, the 90s gave flipped-out forms a back seat. Severe lines and raw materials distinguish many buildings and open spaces. In the large Berlin development of Marzahn Heike Langenbach and Roman Ivancsics pick up the plain geometry of the high-rises constructed in the panel system in their design for Barnim Square.

Trends werden tagesaktuell übernommen und ebensoschnell wieder abgelöst. Allen voran steht die Kaufhauskette Hennes+Mauritz, die alle sechs Wochen ihre komplette Kollektion erneuert. Der Rückzug der Farben und der üppigen Formen fand zu Beginn der 90er Jahre durchweg in allen Branchen statt. In der Mode wurde Überflüssiges radikal abgeschnitten. Es gab Zipper und verdeckte Knopfleisten anstelle auffälliger Knöpfe, Stehkragen anstelle breiter Revers. Schwarz, Anthrazit und Grau sowie strenge Ordnungen bestimmten Kleidung wie Architektur und Außenraum. Natürlich gab es trotzdem leuchtende Farben – sie wurden im Rahmen der Nichtfarben kontrolliert in Szene gesetzt. Natürlich gab es trotzdem Ausgefallenes – man denke an die blattvergoldete Rotunde des Büros Kiefer im Hof der Berliner Reinhardtstraße. Friedliche Koexistenz der Stile und Kombinationsfreude gehören zum Zeitgeist und lassen sich ebensogut in der Modewelt beobachten.

Neben der Form und der Funktion kommt den Materialien als Vermittler von Gestaltung eine entscheidende Rolle zu. Zwei Objekte gleicher Form und Funktion, jedoch unterschiedlichen Materials haben nichts miteinander gemein. Je nachdem, ob man sich beim knielangen Rock für Wolle oder Satin entscheidet, bei der Sitzbank Holz oder Metall wählt, formulieren die Objekte grundverschiedene Aussagen und senden andere Reize. Sehr sinnlich wirken die derzeit getragenen glatten Stoffe und High-Tech-Fasern. Das haptische Erlebnis ist nicht allzu weit entfernt von den glattpolierten, stählernen Fahrradständern, den gummibezogenen Hügeln und den babypopo-glatt geschalten Betonwänden. Gefärbter Beton und farbige Kunststoffbeläge läuten die Renaissance der Farbe ein und bereiten ihrer atmosphärischen Wirkung freie Bahn. Die Zeit des Betons in dezenten Grauschattierungen sowie der Kunststoffbeläge in kategorischem Sportplatz-Rot ist zunächst vorüber. Besonders reizvoll präsentiert sich zudem das Spiel der transparenten Stoffe. Sie verdecken und zeigen, sie schimmern und reflektieren je nach Blickwinkel, Beleuchtung und Inten-

of prominent buttons, and stand-up collars instead of wide lapels. Black, slate and grey as well as severe orders came to determine clothing as well as houses and free spaces. Of course there were still some bright colours. They became strictly controlled focal points within a framework of non-colours. Of course there were still striking effects. Remember the gold leaf rotunda in the inner court of Berlin's Reinhardtstrasse. The peaceful coexistence of styles and the joy of creating combinations belong to the zeitgeist and can be observed in the world of fashion as well.

Besides form and function, materials have a decisive role to play in expressing a design. Two objects with the same form and function but made of different materials have nothing in common. Depending on whether you decide on wool or satin for your knee-length skirt, wood or metal for your bench, the objects formulate fundamentally different messages and awaken different

stimuli. The smooth fabrics and high-tech fibres people are currently wearing seem very sensual. The texture you feel is not all that different from the smoothly polished, steel bicycle racks, the rubber coated hills and the walls made of concrete poured in planed formwork, all as smooth as babies' bottoms. Tinted concrete and coloured plastic covers are heralding a renaissance of colour and giving free rein to the effect of colour on atmosphere. The era of concrete in subtle shades of grey and plastic covers in typical playground red is over for now. Furthermore, there is the particularly appealing play of transparent materials. They cover and expose, they glitter and reflect, depending on your viewpoint, the lighting, and the wearer's intentions. The Dutch design for a double residential court in the large Berlin development of Hohenschönhausen, with a semitransparent metal screen that both separates and links the courts, constitutes an excellent illustration of the art of using such materials. It has been a long time since open space planners have thought about the spatial effects of light as much as in the age of fluorescent sports clothing, blinking running shoes and glittering Lurex shirts.

If you look at materials only in terms of pragmatics, you cannot fail to come across buzzwords such as "multi-functionalism" and "recycling." In fashion this is called "functional workwear" and is clearly defined by Velcro fasteners, tunnel shapes, variably detachable pockets, sleeves and trouser legs. Landscape architects for their part keep quiet about the concrete uses of their flexibly and multi-functionally designed objects and surfaces. The new range of recycled materials is extremely pragmatic. Some applications, such as brick scrap or pulverised coal floors, are very

tion des Trägers. Der holländische Entwurf für einen doppelten Wohnhof in der Berliner Großsiedlung Hohenschönhausen illustriert diese Kunst trefflich mit einem Raumteiler aus schimmerndem, halbtransparentem Lochblech, der die Höfe zugleich trennt und verbindet. Über die räumliche Wirkung von Licht dachten Freiraumplaner ebenfalls lange nicht mehr so

Inszenierte Extravaganz höht den Reiz der strengen Ordnung. Wo kein überflüssiger Knopf das lange Schwarze ziert, darf ein leuchtendes Foulard darüber wehen. Wo ein Hinterhof in der Berliner Reinhardtstraße ganz einfach karg bleibt, wagen die Landschaftsarchitekten des Büros Kiefer eine blattvergoldete Rotunde über der Tiefgarage.

Staged extravagance increases the appeal of severity. While not a single extra button graces the little black dress, a colourful scarf may float above. While the backyard in Berlin's Reinhardtstrasse is still a plain ordinary backyard, the Kiefer office landscape architects dared to place a rotunda in gold foil on top of the underground car park.

good and convincing trailblazing examples. With experiments such as yoghurt cup furniture, however, you wish for nothing more than that competent designers get to work at last so as not to leave the field over to ecologists, chemists and budget auditors without a fight.

Between design ideas and built results, however, there is a huge gap in Germany. You begin to worry that future generations will have to find the really good ideas in landscape architecture of the turn of the century in the professional journals. These publications present projects from abroad, where, as we know, everything is always better. There is no doubt that clients abroad are more willing to take risks, even though the unavoidable failures of experimental design have sometimes been mistaken for sloppy construction. Moreover, many a good idea fails in the face of contractors and building material manufacturers not interested in innovation. After all, in practice demand is what dictates production and prices. Many a custom-made item thus becomes unaffordable and remains nothing but a fantasy on paper.

Nonetheless, today's planners enjoy experimenting and are open to technical innovations. They stubbornly develop good ideas. Moreover, their approach to materials has become more playful. And why should garbage, advertising, slide projections or even fish (as planned at the Lehrter Bahnhof railway station in Berlin) not become conventional materials to design with in open spaces? Whether you are dealing with transparent nylon shirts, Polartec pullovers and see-through camisole straps in fashion, or gold leaf, plastic and fish in open spaces, the motto is: "anything goes." And that arouses our curiosity.

intensiv nach wie zu Zeiten der fluoreszierenden Sportjacken, der blinkenden Turnschuhe und der glitzernden Lurex-Shirts.

Betrachtet man die Materialien einmal ganz pragmatisch, stößt man unweigerlich auf Schlagworte wie »Multifunktionalität« und »Recycling«. In der Mode heißt das »functional workwear« und ist mit all den Klettverschlüssen, Tunnelzügen, flexibel abknöpfbaren Taschen, Ärmeln und Hosenbeinen klar definiert. Die Landschaftsarchitekten hingegen schweigen sich über die konkreten Nutzungen ihrer flexibel und multifunktional geschaffenen Objekte und Flächen aus. Äußerst pragmatisch erscheint da die neue Palette von Recyclingmaterialien. Manche Anwendungen, etwa Ziegelbruchflächen oder Kohlenstaubtennen, weisen als sehr gute und überzeugende Beispiele den Weg. Bei Experimenten wie Tischen aus recycelten Joghurtbechern wünscht man sich allerdings nichts sehnlicher, als dass endlich kompetente Gestalter ans Werk gehen, um das Feld nicht kampflos den Ökologen, Chemikern und Wirtschaftsberatern zu überlassen.

Zwischen den Entwurfsideen und den gebauten Ergebnissen klafft in Deutschland noch eine große Lücke. Man muss befürchten, dass sich künftige Generationen die wirklich guten Ideen der Landschaftsarchitektur der Jahrtausendwende aus Fachzeitschriften erschließen müssen. Denn die zeigen Beispiele von anderswo, und dort ist es bekanntlich immer besser – man denke an die strapazierten Vorbilder Barcelona und Holland. Zweifellos besitzen die Bauherren dort mehr Mut zum Risiko, auch wenn mitunter die unvermeidlichen Fehlschläge experimenteller Gestaltung mit Unvermögen oder Schlamperei am Bau verwechselt werden. Manch gute Idee scheitert zudem an der mangelnden Innovationslust der ausführenden Firmen und Baustoffhersteller. In der Praxis diktiert schließlich die Nachfrage Produktion und Preis. Entsprechend unerschwinglich wird dann so manche Sonderanfertigung und bleibt Fantasie auf dem Papier.

Trotzdem sind die Planerinnen und Planer von heute experimentierfreudig und offen für technische Neuerungen. Sie entwickeln hartnäckig gute Ideen. Ihr Umgang mit Materialien ist zudem spielerischer geworden. Warum sollten nicht auch Müll, Werbung, Lichtbild-Projektionen oder echte Fische, wie am Lehrter Bahnhof in Berlin geplant, als konventionelle Gestaltungsmittel für den Freiraum herhalten? Ob nun transparente Nylonshirts, Polartec-Pullover und durchsichtige Hemdchen-Träger in der Mode, oder Blattgold, Kunststoff und Fische im Freiraum – »anything goes« heißt das Motto. Und das macht neugierig.

Tilburg: Magnolien im Schieferbeet

Tiburg: Magnolias in a bed of slate

Adriaan Geuze

Der Garten einer Versicherungsfirma lädt Mitarbeiter wie Anwohner an seine Wasser-Tische und auf seine Rasen- und Schieferplateaus.

The garden of an insurance company lures employees and nearby dwellers to its tables of water and its lawn and slate plateaus.

Der Hauptsitz der Interpolis-Versicherung liegt in der Achse des Tilburger Bahnhofs. Das Gebäude ragt im Norden eines dreieckigen Grundstücks auf und lässt Raum für einen etwa zwei Hektar großen Garten. Wir gestalteten ihn als einen ruhigen, introvertierten Ort, von der Umgebung abgeschlossen durch Hecken und einen dunkelgrünen Stahlzaun mit stilisierten Stechpalmen-Blättern. Tagsüber steht der Garten den Mitarbeiterinnen und Mitarbeitern der Firma ebenso offen wie den Tilburger Bürgern. Das Verwaltungsgebäude des Architekten Abe Bonnema forderte eine Gartengestaltung, die ihm etwas entgegensetzen würde. Wir pflanzten deshalb Douglasien in lockeren Gruppen. Ihre langen, schmalen Schatten bieten dem Hochhaus Paroli. Die Rasenflächen erscheinen als tektonische Platten, gerahmt von dunkelgrauen Stützmauern aus Be-

The headquarters of the Interpolis insurance company is located on the axis of the Tilburg railway station. The building rises in the north of a triangular plot, and leaves enough space for a garden of about two hectares in size. We designed it as a quiet, introverted place sealed off from its surroundings by hedges and a dark green steel

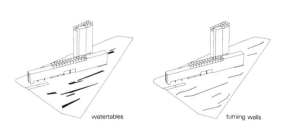

watertables   turning walls

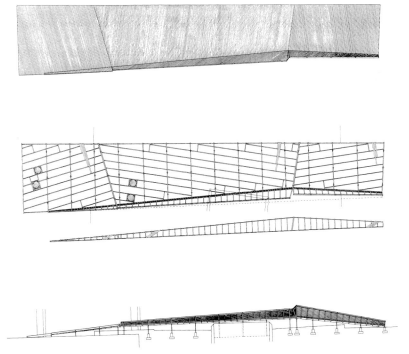

fence with stylised holly leaf ornaments. During the day the garden is open to the employees of the company as well as to the people of Tilburg. The administration building of the architect Abe Bonnema called for a garden design which stood in contrast to it. Therefore we planted Douglas firs in loose clusters. Their long, narrow shadows easily stand up to the building. The lawn areas look like tectonic plates framed by dark grey supporting walls of concrete. The long extended tables of water, the shortest of which measures 20 metres and the longest 85 metres, are especially eye-catching. Together with their water lilies they offer a habitat for frogs. The stage-like, non-parallel arrangement of the basins continuously opens up new impressive sight lines to the visitor. Soft footpaths covered with red-brown mulch lead through the garden. On their way visitors find places to rest here and there on the wide rims of the tables of water or upon the wood-topped supporting walls. The employees can even work outdoors here on their laptops which have a wireless link to the intranet of the company.

At the foot of the building we designed a plateau made of plates of slate. Laid out according to different angles they form tectonic plates similar to the lawn areas. In spring the light-coloured blossoms of the Magnolia trees present a marked contrast to the massive, dark, rough

Vom Dach des Bürohochhauses lässt sich die Tektonik des Gartens mit Elementen aus Rasen, Wasser, Mulch und Schiefer gut erkennen. Douglasien mit ihren langen, schwarzen Schatten setzen dem Hochhaus klare Vegetationsvolumina entgegen. Als repräsentativer Eingang überbrückt ein mehrfach geknickter Steg (Pläne links) die Schieferfläche am Fuße des Gebäudes.
From the roof of the office high-rise the structure of the garden with its lawn, water, turf and slate elements can be easily identified. Douglas firs with their long, black shadows set distinct volumes of vegetation over and against the high-rise building.
Forming the representative entrance a footbridge with several bends (plans, left) spans the slate area at the base of the building.

ton. Besonders auffällig sind die langgestreckten »Wasser-Tische«, deren kleinster 20 Meter und deren größter 85 Meter in der Länge misst. Mit ihren Wasserlilien bieten sie einen Lebensraum für Frösche. Die kulissenartige, nicht-parallele Anordnung der Becken eröffnet den Besuchern immer wieder neue, starke Blickachsen. Weiche, mit rotbraunem Mulch bedeckte Fußwege führen durch den Garten – auf ihrem Weg finden die Besucher hier und da Plätze zum Ausruhen auf den breiten Rändern der Wasser-Ti-

slate plateau

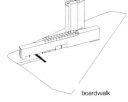

boardwalk

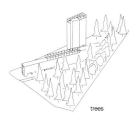

trees

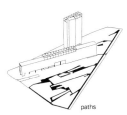

paths

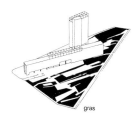

gras

hedge/entrance

sche oder auf den holzgedeckten Stützmauern. Der Garten soll der Erholung und der Muße dienen, aber man kann in ihm auch arbeiten: Die Versicherungsangestellten können sich mit ihrem kabellos ans Intranet der Firma gekoppelten Laptop einen Arbeitsplatz im Grünen suchen.

Am Fuße des Gebäudes gestalteten wir ein Plateau aus großen Schieferplatten. In verschiedenen Winkeln verlegt, formen sie ähnlich wie die Rasenflächen tektonische Platten. Im Frühjahr bilden die duftigen, hellen Blüten der Ma-

gnolienbäume einen auffälligen Kontrast zu dem massiven, rauhen, scharfkantigen und dunklen Schiefer. Vom Gebäude leitet eine Holzbrücke über das Schieferplateau zur Eingangsebene des Gartens. Zusätzlich zu den zwei Toren im Metallzaun bildet dieser Platz den dritten, repräsentativen Eingang zum Garten.

and sharp-edged slate. There is a wooden bridge that leads from the building over the slate plateau to the place of entry into the garden. This place forms a third more presentable entrance in addition to the other two in the metal fence.

Interpolis Garden, Tilburg, The Netherlands
Client: Interpolis Verzekeringsmaatschappij
Design: West 8 landscape architects and urban planners, Rotterdam
Size: 2 hectares
Planning: 1997
Construction: 1998

Im Frühjahr heben sich die zarten Magnolienblüten vom scharfkantigen Schiefer ab. Die kantigen Betonmauern setzen sich deutlich von den weichen Mulchbeeten ab.

In spring the delicate Magnolia blossoms present a marked contrast with the sharp-edged slate. The edged concrete walls purposely contrasts with the soft mulch flower beds.

Neapel: Materialtest für den Städtebau

Naples: Makeshift materials as urban development strategy

Stefano Boeri

In Naples, efforts are underway to refurbish the city's bustling passenger port. At Beverello Pier, an area next to the densest part of the historical city, our office has been experimenting with a new urban development strategy. In this, our objectives have been to increase the size of the area set aside for the passengers embarking on the numerous ferries, and at the same time to create contemporary collective spaces for the incredibly crowded city. Our solution was to propose three plans of action, and instead of carrying them out chronologically, as in the usual course of events, to work on them simultaneously. The intention of this approach is to simultaneously deal with various levels of discourse involving different interlocutors. The three plans have been or are be-

Mit unserem Umgestaltungsprojekt für den Neapolitaner Hafen probierten wir eine neue Strategie aus. Dort, wo der Hafen an den dichtesten Teil der Altstadt grenzt, schlugen wir vor, zeitgenössisch gestaltete öffentliche Freiräume zu entwickeln und den Besuchern der Stadt mehr Platz anzubieten. Der historische Kern Neapels hat solche offenen Flächen bitter nötig. Um das Projekt voranzutreiben, starteten wir zeitgleich drei Aktionen, die normalerweise aufeinander folgen. Auf ein und demselben Grundstück, nämlich dem Zugang des Passagierschiff-Anlegers, entwickelten wir drei Projekte: einen Entwurf zur städtischen Erneuerung für das gesamte Areal, einen Entwurf für einen neuen Terminal, und schließlich einen ausführungsreifen Plan für eine provisorische Promenade anstelle der Mauer, die bisher den Hafen vom Maschio-Angioino-Schloss und der Altstadt trennte. Hinter diesem Vorgehen steht der Gedanke, simultan

Zeitgleich mit den Plänen für die Hafenumgestaltung entstand eine provisorische Promenade, die den Fortgang des Projekts fordert.

A temporary promenade built as part of the renovation of the Italian city's port area is to ensure continuation of the project.

Am Beverello-Pier stößt die enge Altstadt Neapels an den Hafen. Nachdem die Mauern um den Hafen gefallen sind, schlagen die Architekten vom Studio Boeri vor, hier die Stadt neu zu gestalten, mit öffentlichen Freiräumen und einem neuen Passagierterminal.

The Beverello Pier is where crowded historic Naples meets the harbour. Now that the walls around the harbour have been demolished, the Boeri office's architects propose redesigning this part of town with public spaces and a new passenger terminal.

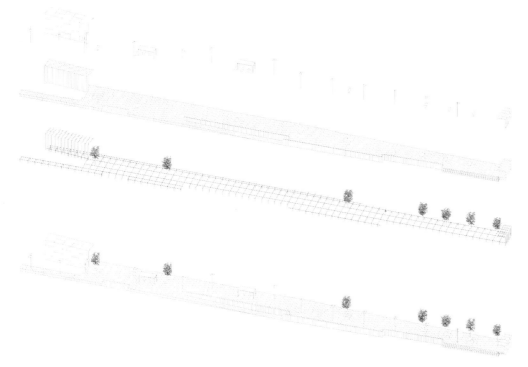

ing implemented on the same portion of land, and consist of an urban renovation project that covers the entire passenger embarkation section, an architectural project for the central area, and creation of a temporary public fixture. This is to replace the wall that separated the port from the city and the Maschio Angioino castle.

The temporary fixture consists of a wooden deck 15 meters wide and 150 meters long, and is deliberately made of low-budget materials, such as wooden construction planks and scaffolding pipes – all elements that can easily be dismantled and assembled again elsewhere. Besides serving as a balcony above the port, it suggests a possible new relationship between the port and city.

The deliberately makeshift character of the promenade, as demonstrated by the choice of building materials, is a reminder of the passage of time and all the delays and detours that have taken place since the beginning of the renovation plan. This makes the process involved, one that could easily be impeded by numerous obstacles, an irreversible one, and helps ensure the transformation begun by the other two projects.

auf verschiedenen Niveaus der Planung zu agieren und einen Diskurs mit den unterschiedlichen Planungsakteuren in Gang zu bringen.

Inzwischen ersetzt eine 15 Meter breite und 150 Meter lange Promenade aus Holz die alte Hafenmauer am Beverello-Pier. Die Promenade ähnelt einem Rettungsschiff, das die Grenze zwischen Hafen und Stadt nachzeichnet. Die Materialien, Schalungsholz und Baugerüstrohre, sind ausgesprochen günstig und lassen sich leicht ab- und anderswo wieder aufbauen. Die Promenade verschafft der Stadt einen Balkon am Hafen, und zudem führt sie im Maßstab eins zu eins vor, wie Stadt und Hafen miteinander verbunden werden können. Ihre Existenz macht es geradezu unmöglich, die nächsten Entwicklungsschritte zu vergessen, die wir in den beiden anderen Projekten vorgeschlagen haben. Auf dem Material des Provisoriums lässt sich wie auf einer Uhr die Zeit ablesen, die seit Planungsbeginn verstrichen ist. Das Material misst Verzögerungen, zeichnet Warteschleifen auf und verhindert Rückzieher, die ansonsten oft das Aus für Projekte dieser Größenordnung bedeuten.

Aus drei Schichten besteht die provisorische Promenade am Beverello-Pier: einer Struktur aus Baugerüst-Rohren, einer Verkleidung aus Schalungsholz und städtischem Mobiliar. Ihre Materialien sind extrem günstig, wiederverwendbar und bilden für die Zeit ihres Bestehens einen reizvollen Kontrast zu den alten Mauern der Maschio-Angioino-Burg.

The temporary promenade along the Beverello Pier consists of three layers: a structure made of scaffolding pipes, a cladding of planks, and urban furniture. The materials are very inexpensive, re-usable, and for the duration of their use they provide an attractive contrast to the old walls of the Maschio Angioino castle.

Zum Meer hin ist der Unterstand der Promenade mit einfachem Walzblech verkleidet. Die ausdrücklich provisorische Gestaltung führt den Neapolitanern täglich im Maßstab eins zu eins vor Augen, dass der nächste Entwicklungsschritt des öffentlichen Raumes noch bevorsteht. Wie sich Stadt und Hafen miteinander verbinden lassen, können sie schon jetzt hautnah erleben.

Facing the sea, the shelter over the promenade is clad in plain rolled sheet metal. The deliberately temporary design shows the Neapolitans every day on a one-to-one scale that the next step in public space development is still to come. At this point they can already experience in person how the port and the city can be interlinked.

Temporary passenger platform at Beverello Pier, Naples, Italy
Client: Port Authority of Naples
Master project: Stefano Boeri with Gianandrea Barreca, Nicola Bianchi, Luca Bucci, Giovanni La Varra, Claudio Finaldi Russo
Size: 1,400 square metres
Planning: 1998
Construction: 1998
Costs: ITL 410 million

Basel: Feigenernte an der Schönaustraße

Basel: A harvest of figs at Schönaustrasse

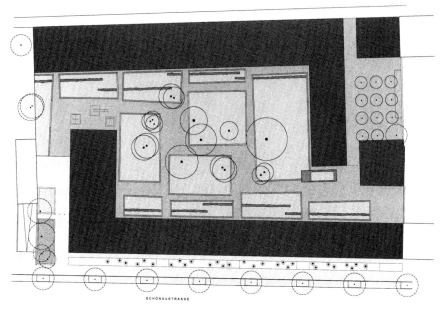

Stefan Rotzler
Matthias Krebs

Materials pushed to their limits and beyond, materials that lose in seriousness when placed in startling combinations, as in the theory of wit put forward by Sigmund Freud. This explains jokes as being stories that unexpectedly bring together two incompatible situations or ideas, thus surprising the listener and leading to a build-up of inner tension which is discharged in laughter. Does this mean that unexpected combinations of materials should be seen as a sort of joke? Not at all. In our case, we put materials together in an unusual way to evince an amused chuckle and thus create a light-hearted mood.

An apartment complex involving considerable budget constraints was recently completed at Schönaustrasse on the edge of Kleinbasel, a district of the Swiss city of Basel close to the Trade Fair Centre and Deutsche Bundesbahn property. In the complex, two angular buildings, placed not quite parallel to each other, make up an urban ensemble with a contiguous courtyard area. The buildings thus form a sort of protective enclosure, to which residents can repair to enjoy the peace and quiet and the group of trees that provides the court with a colourful focal point. The trees, which can be seen from all the apartments, consist of maple species from all over the world, including ornamental Asian species such as bizarre red snake-bark maple and ash-leaved maple (box elder) from Japan and paperbark maple from China, as well as a swiftly-growing silver maple from North America. Indigenous mountain, Norway and field maples round off the group to create a more down-to-earth effect.

The ground surface consists of a carpet made up of pathways and slightly raised lawn rectangles that seem to hover over the ground. As a result,

Materialien, die an ihre Grenzen gehen und noch ein bisschen darüber hinaus... Materialien, die in Kombination miteinander den Ernst abwerfen und über sich selber lachen... Vielleicht spiegelt sich in diesen Andeutungen etwas von dem wider, was Sigmund Freud in seiner Theorie des Witzes auslotete: Nach ihm besteht der Reiz des Witzes darin, dass auf zunächst bierernste Weise Dinge gegenüber gestellt werden, die an sich gar nichts miteinander zu tun haben. Ihr unerwartetes Zusammentreffen an einem erstaunlichen Ort zu einer unerwarteten Zeit setzt durch den Überrumpelungseffekt beim Zuhörer psychische Energie frei, die sich in einem herzhaften Lachen äußert. Der Witz hat gesessen. Materialisierung als Witz verstanden? Selbstverständlich nicht. Vielmehr sollten Materialien Leichtigkeit vermitteln, ein befreiendes Lächeln oder gar Lachen hervorrufen.

Am Rande von Kleinbasel ist in Nachbarschaft zur Messe Basel und zu den Gleisen der Deutschen Bundesbahn unter großem Kostendruck kürzlich die Wohnanlage Schönaustraße

Im Hof des Wohnkomplexes bilden Rasenfelder den Untergrund für Ahorne aus aller Welt, im Vorgarten wachsen Feigen in Chromstahltöpfen. At a new residential complex, maple species from all over the world grow in areas of lawn, and figs burgeon in chromium steel planters.

Geometrisch leicht gegeneinander verschobene Rasengevierte ordnen den Hof. Durch die breiten Betoneinfassungen wirken die Wege wie eingeschnitten. Vor den Erdgeschosswohnungen wächst Miscanthus in Bändern, und schützt vor Einblicken. Ein kissenartig geformtes Brunnen-Objekt schmückt die fensterlose Wand an der engsten Stelle des Hofes.

Slightly staggered geometrically, rectangular lawns organise the court. Thick concrete borders make the pathways between them look cut out. Rows of miscanthus growing in front of the ground floor flats shield them from view. A pillow-shaped work of art forms a fountain that decorates the windowless wall at the narrowest part of the court.

the gravel pathways, which get narrower and wider in successive waves, seem scored into the ground like the lines of a woodcut. The rims of the lawn sections are made of black, pre-cast concrete beams that widen into benches here and there. Linear lighting fixtures cast incidental light onto the paths, which feature red marl gravel from the Black Forest, while ribbons of grass and miscanthus species create filigree screens between the communal parts of the courtyard and the ground-storey apartments, thus discouraging any invasion of privacy.

A water basin faced in blue plastic matting to create a cushion-like effect introduces an element of drama at the southern-facing and narrowest part of the courtyard. A normal droplight shines on the water at night, creating dancing reflections on a windowless facade.

fertiggestellt worden. Zwei winkelförmige Baukörper fügen sich zu einem urbanen Ensemble mit fließendem Hofraum. Im Schutz der Häuser lassen sich hier Ruhe und Nähe der Bäume genießen. Von allen Wohnungen aus sichtbar steht eine Ahorn-Gruppe mit Arten aus aller Welt als Blickfang im Zentrum des Hofes. Zimt-Ahorn aus China, bizarrer Schlangenhaut-Ahorn und feinblättriger Fächer-Ahorn aus Japan vertreten die ornamentalen asiatischen Ahornarten. Aus Nordamerika stammt der raschwüchsige Silber-Ahorn. Einheimisch sind Berg-, Spitz- und Feldahorn.

Der Hof besitzt einen steinernen »Grundteppich«. In ihrer Geometrie leicht verschobene Rasengevierte schweben als leicht erhabene Felder im Hofraum. Wege und Plätze wirken holzschnittartig eingekerbt. Sie verengen und verbreitern sich peristaltisch. Die Einfassungen der Rasengevierte sind aus vorgefertigten schwarzen Betonbalken gefügt. An manchen Orten werden sie zu langen Sitzbänken. Lineare Lichtbänder werfen Streiflicht über den rötlichen wassergebundenen Schwarzwaldmergel. Als filigrane Vorhänge wachsen parallel zu den Erdgeschosswohnungen Grasbänder mit Miscanthus-Arten. Sie schaffen eine Schwelle zum privaten Raum und mindern unerwünschte Einblicke.

Courtyard of the Schönaustrasse residential complex, Basel, Switzerland
Client: Pension Fund of Basel State Employees
Architects: Proplaning AG, Basel
Landscape architects: Rotzler Krebs Partner, Gockhausen/Winterthur, Switzerland
Water basin artists: Claudia Müller and Julia Müller, Basel
Size: 6,000 square metres
Planning: 1997 – 1999
Construction: 1999 – 2000
Costs: SFR 840,000

Ein mit Kunststoffmatten blau verkleidetes, kissenartig geformtes Wasserbecken dramatisiert die nach Süden orientierte, enge Stelle des Hofes. Eine gewöhnliche Pendelleuchte wirft des Nachts ihren Schein auf das Wasserbecken, und das Wasser reflektiert tänzelnde Wasserkringel an eine fensterlose Hauswand.

The area facing the street has the appearance of an abstract "green space". Thyme grows in the joints of mosaic slabs of green Swiss granite, placed to mark the boundary between the property and the pavement. In the unusual combina-

Grüner Andeer Granit bildet ein Band zwischen der Südfassade und dem Gehweg des Kleinbasler Wohnkomplexes. Thymian in den Fugen der Mosaikplatten und winterharte Feigen in den Chromstahltöpfen schaffen eine mediterrane Atmosphäre.

Green granite from Andeer forms a band between the south facade and a pathway in a residential ensemble in Lesser Basel. Thyme in the joints between mosaic slabs and winter-hardy figs in chromium steel pots create a Mediterranean atmosphere.

tion referred to above, fig bushes have been planted out in the front in chromium steel troughs,
which are placed in horizontal lines to underscore
the slight slope. The first crop of figs was produced this summer.

An der Straße liegt eine abstrakte »Grünfläche«: Mosaikplatten aus grü-
nem Andeer Granit trennen den Gehweg von der Fassade. In den Fugen
wächst Thymian. Chromstahltröge mit exakt horizontalem Rand betonen
das leichte Gefälle der Straße. Sie sind mit winterharten Feigensträuchern
bepflanzt – schon in diesem Sommer wurden die ersten Feigen geerntet.

Im Innenhof erzeugen asiati-
sche Ahornarten exotische Bilder. Die Gehwege aus rötli-
chem Schwarzwaldmergel kon-
trastieren mit dem Grün der
Rasenrechtecke. Des Nachts
höht Kunstlicht die Geometrie
des Hofes, die Leuchten sind in
die Betonbänke integriert.

Asian species of maple create
exotic scenes in the inner
court. Reddish marl on the
pathways contrasts with the
green of the rectangular lawns.
At night artificial light underscores the geometry of the
court; the lighting is integrated into the concrete benches.

Genf: Erinnerung in Stein

Geneva: Memories in stone

Giordano Tironi

As the name Jardin des Minoteries, mill garden, already suggests this little park is located in an area of former mills alongside a stream - today an urban housing area in the larger city region of Geneva. New multi-storeyed buildings characterize the location. In designing the garden these features as well as the underground garage extending underneath the garden had to be adequately taken into account. Directed views determine the design, and connect a row of closed outdoor spaces: The pergola, the boule-alley, the rain shelter, the well site – all semi-public spaces which allow for retreat as well as togetherness in many forms. They offer room for both dwellers and visitors, for the young and the old, and for diverse activities and needs. In this way open space helps to overcome the differences among human beings without doing away with them altogether.

Since the small park is closed on all sides, it is not supposed to reveal itself to the observer upon first glance, but rather gradually step by step. This makes it appear larger than it really is. For example, the gentle elevation along the lawn in the centre covers up one's view of the building foundations. They, in turn, appear lighter once the view of their line of contact with the ground has become obscured. Also, the sequence of the wall disks serves to widen up space. The array absorbs one's attention. One's glance passes from wall to wall, and thus explores the garden space at a slower pace. The play with light and shade upon the different materials supports this kind of differentiated perception.

Originally, the area designated for the park hardly showed any more signs of history. It was as if history had been obliterated, or in better words: ploughed under by a machine designed to

Mauern, Vegetation und Fußwege zeigen die Spuren der Geschichte im Jardin des Minoteries, einem ehemaligen Mühlenstandort.

Walls, vegetation and paths display traces of history in the Jardin des Minoteries – the former site of a mill.

Wie der Name Jardin des Minoteries, Mühlengarten, schon verrät, liegt dieser kleine Park auf dem Gebiet ehemaliger Mühlenbetriebe an einem Bach – heute ein städtisches Wohnviertel im Großraum Genf. Mehrgeschossige Neubauten prägen den Ort und wollten bei der Gestaltung des Gartens ebenso berücksichtigt sein wie die Tiefgarage, die sich unter der Freifläche erstreckt. Blickachsen bestimmen den Entwurf für den Park und verbinden eine Reihe »Kammern« unter freiem Himmel: die Pergola, den Boule-Platz, den Unterstand, den Brunnenplatz – halböffentliche Orte, die Rückzug und Gemeinsamkeit in vielen Formen zulassen. Sie bieten Raum für Bewohner wie Besucher, für Junge und Alte und für

Mauern und Bänke des Parks nehmen alte Flurmuster auf. So ergibt sich auf dem steinernen Platz ein spannungsvolles Arrangement mit einem doppelten Brunnen: Auf der einen Seite sieht und hört man das Wasser ins Bassin sprudeln, auf der anderen kann man es direkt aus dem Hahn trinken.

Walls and benches of the park reflect the old field patterns. The result is a scintillating arrangement with a double fountain on the stone-surfaced square: To the one side you hear the water gurgling in the basin, on the other you can turn on the tap and have a drink.

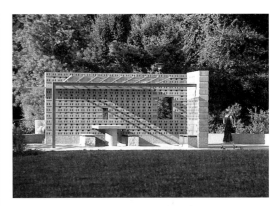

make us forget time. Therefore, the idea to search for the hidden memories of the location and to look for traces of reminiscences in the scanty remains – low walls, lines of vegetation made up of trees, hedges and paths – which have escaped the onslaught of urbanization immediately struck one's mind. The park design is oriented upon these discrete elements of the landscape which happen to be much more important as witnesses of the location's history than the buildings. That which the city swallowed up now reappears again, but without any nostalgic touch to it. Nature in the sense of the urban environment has

vielfältige Tätigkeiten und Bedürfnisse. So hilft der Freiraum, Unterschiede zwischen den Menschen zu überwinden, ohne sie aufzuheben.

Da der kleine Park zu fast allen Seiten geschlossen ist, sollte er sich den Betrachtern nicht auf einen Blick erschließen, sondern nach und nach. Das lässt ihn größer erscheinen. So verdeckt zum Beispiel die leichte Rasenwelle im Zentrum die Sockel der Gebäude. Sie wirken leichter, wenn ihr Kontaktpunkt mit dem Boden verdeckt ist. Auch die Abfolge der Mauerscheiben dient dazu, den Raum zu weiten. Ihre Staffelung hält den Blick auf. Er gleitet von Mauer zu Mauer und erfasst den Gartenraum langsamer. Das Spiel von Licht und Schatten auf den Materialien unterstützt diese differenzierte Wahrnehmung.

Das Gelände, das für die Anlage des Parks vorgesehen war, zeigte kaum mehr Spuren der Geschichte. Sie war wie ausgelöscht, oder besser: wie un-

Holzplanken laden zum Sitzen auf der Dreierbank ein, Lochblech rahmt die Eingangspasserelle, Hohlblocksteine bilden den Rücken des Unterstandes, filigrane Edelstahlrohre und Drähte überspannen als Pergola einen Sitzplatz in der Rasenfläche. Alle Materialien wirken durch ihre Nuancen der Farbe Grau.

Wooden planks invite you to sit down on the three-seated bench, punched metal foil frames the entry passage. Hollow blocks of stone form the back of the shelter, filigree high-grade steel pipes and wires form a pergola spanning over a seat. All of the materials reflect their fine nuances of the colour grey.

tergepflügt von einer Maschine zum Vergessen der Zeit. Deshalb drängte sich die Suche auf nach dem Gedächtnis des Ortes, nach Spuren der Erinnerung in den bescheidenen Resten, die der fortschreitenden Verstädterung entkommen waren: niedrige Mauern, Vegetationslinien aus Bäumen und Hecken, Wege... Die Gestaltung des Parks orientiert sich an diesen diskre-

always had to cope with the grey appearance of buildings. For about twenty years we have been experiencing the buildings becoming more colourful, but not always necessarily to their advantage. All too often we are confronted with a

ten Elementen der Landschaft, die viel stärker als die Bauten von der Geschichte des Ortes zeugen. Das, was die Stadt verschluckte, kommt nun wieder zum Vorschein, und zwar ohne Nostalgie.

Schon immer hat sich die städtische Natur mit dem Grau der Gebäude arrangieren müssen. Seit ungefähr zwanzig Jahren erleben wir, wie die Bauten immer farbiger werden – aber nicht unbedingt zu ihrem Vorteil. Allzu oft stehen wir vor einer Farborgie, die eine Wahrnehmung des Gesamtbildes erschwert. Kann man einen Garten in Grautönen gestalten? Vor den dunklen, massigen Neubauten mit ihren unentschiedenen Farben wirken die hellen Töne des Pflasters und der Gartenmauern wie eine diskrete Nuance der Vegetation. Sie beruhigen das aufgezwungene Durcheinander der umgebenden Gebäude. Beläge und Gehwegkanten aus Naturstein sind kostenlose Recycling-Ware und wurden während des Baus vor Ort gefun-

multicoloured kakophony that interferes with the perception of the whole picture. In the same vein one might ask: Could one possibly design a garden in shades of grey?

In contrast to the dark, massive modern buildings with their indecisive colours the light shades of the cobble stones and garden walls appear as a discreet nuance to the vegetation. They quiet down the imposing helter-skelter of the surrounding buildings. Pavements and rims of foot paths made of natural rocks are cost-free recycling goods, and were found on site in the wake of building construction, or were transported

Recycelte Steinplatten helfen die Materialkosten zu reduzieren und verleihen dem Ort von Anfang an eine vertraute Atmosphäre. Waschbeton wählten die Planer, weil das Licht auf seiner rauhen Oberfläche ein besonders schönes Spiel erzeugt.

Recycled stone plates help to reduce the costs, and provide the place with an atmosphere of familiarity right from the outset. The planners chose pebbled concrete, because the light shining on its rough surface displays an especially beautiful effect.

from the depots of Geneva's urban construction agency. The granit benches for the rain shelter, for example, used to serve as bases for 19th century archways. The vertical square blocks of the boule-alley used to form the steps to an old, later

destroyed chapel. All of these materials used to belong to other parts of the city. They had become useless, and have now found a new, fulfilling use within the Jardin des Minoteries. In order to invent something new, one has to start from that which exists. For, building blocks of the old city liven up the new city.

We chose the keepsakes in stone according to their appearance under the light, and not because of their form. In the garden they usually show their hidden aspects which no-one has hitherto caught a glimpse of. In a heap of other materials we found the granite table for the rain shelter. It

den oder aus den Lagern des Genfer Baureferats geholt. So dienten die Granit-Bänke des Unterstands einst als Sockel für Torbögen des 19. Jahrhunderts, die vertikalen Kantsteine des Boule-Platzes formten als Stufen den Aufgang zu einer alten, später zerstörten Kapelle. Alle diese Materialien gehörten zuvor anderen Teilen der Stadt. Sie waren unnütz geworden und finden nun im Jardin des Minoteries eine neue, angemessene Verwendung. Um etwas Neues zu erfinden, muss man vom Bestehenden ausgehen. Denn Bausteine der alten Stadt beleben die neue.

Die steinernen Erinnerungsstücke wählten wir wegen ihrer Erscheinung unter dem Licht, nicht wegen ihrer Form. Im Garten zeigen sie größtenteils ihre versteckte Seite, die niemand bisher zu Gesicht bekam. In einem Haufen anderer Materialien fanden wir den Granittisch des Unterstandes. Er zeigt die Spuren der Zeit und der Nutzungen, zum Beispiel Rillen, die rieselndes Wasser auf der Oberfläche hinterlassen hat. Die Zeit prägt die Materialien besser als wir – lassen wir sie gewähren. In der Architektur kommt es nicht darauf an, ob Beton jung ist oder alt. Im

Park hingegen ist die Oberfläche vieler Mauern und Böden so bearbeitet worden, dass sie »alt« erscheint. Das Licht »gräbt« sich in ihre Unebenheiten, so als ob sie schon immer da gewesen wären.

Bis ins 19. Jahrhundert bestimmte der Kampf zwischen der Stadt und dem Wasser des Bachs das Gelände des Jardin des Minoteries. Aus technischen Gründen ließ sich im Park kein Wasserlauf realisieren, der an das gezähmte Wasser erinnert, das früher auf die Mühlen lief. Deshalb schnitten wir aus einer blauen Marmorplatte, Azul Macauba genannt, 16 Quadrate von zehn mal zehn Zentimeter und ordneten sie in einer Linie auf einer Mauer an. Die durchlaufenden Adern des Marmors erinnern an ein Wasserrinnsal. Die Linie liegt auf derselben Höhe wie der Trinkwasserauslass des Brunnens am Ende der Mauer. Eine Platte aus Azul Macauba leitet das Wasser ins Becken. Gerade bei grauem Wetter fehlt dem Wasser oft Farbe –

Anstelle eines echten Wasserlaufes symbolisierten die Planer das Wasser mit einer Reihe bläulicher Quadrate aus Azul-Macauba-Marmor, die in regelmäßigen Abständen in eine Mauer eingelassen sind. Sie führt zu einem Wasserauslass. Über eine blaue Marmorplatte läuft dort das Wasser ins Bassin.

It was technically impossible to conduct a watercourse through the park. So the planners symbolised the water by an array of bluish squares of Azul Macauba marble which have been inserted into the wall at regular intervals. It leads to a water outlet. There the water flows over a blue marble plate into the basin.

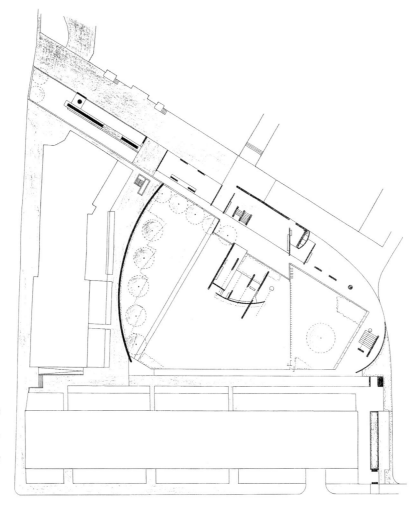

Eine große Rasenfläche bildet das Zentrum des Parks zwischen den Hochhausriegeln. Die Pergola leitet zur steinernen Schiene mit Sitzplätzen und Brunnen über. Als Fluchtpunkt dient der Unterstand an einer Spitze des dreieckigen Grundstücks.

A large lawn area forms the centre of the park between the rows of houses. The pergola leads over to a stone slab with seats and fountains. The shelter at the end of the triangular site serves as a focal point of one's view.

displays the traces of the times when it was used, for example grooves which running water has left behind upon its surface. Time forms the materials better than we can if we let it work. In architecture it does not matter whether concrete is recent or old. In the park on the other hand the surfaces of many walls have been worked upon to such an extent that they appear old. The light "digs" into the uneven surfaces as if they had always been there.

The struggle between the city and the stream's water has determined the terrain well into the 19th century. For technical reasons no watercourse through the park could be realized capable of reminding us of the tamed water that used to run through the mills. Therefore we cut out 16 squares, ten by ten centimetres in size, out of a plate of blue marble called Azul Macauba, and arranged them along a line upon a wall. The traversing veins of the marble remind us of rivulets of water. The height of the line corresponds to that of the outlet for drinking water from the well at the end of the wall. A plate of Azul Macauba conducts the water into the basin. Especially under grey skies the water often lacks colour. In this case the blue of the marble adds a special colouring effect next to the grey shades of the sky and the concrete, and forms a soothing contrast to the colours of the buildings. When dry the marble tiles display a light, discreet blue. Under water or during the rain they change into lively patterns of colourful swabs. Apart from this the park appears to be almost monochrome which enhances one's experience of the changes that time has wrought upon the materials. For, in the end, writes George Kubler, "the forms time has created are the booty we all are trying to get a hold of ".

in diesem Fall fügt das Blau des Marmors dem Himmel und dem Beton einen Akzent hinzu und setzt sich von den zu starken Farben der Neubauten ab. In trockenem Zustand zeigen die Marmorfliesen ein helles, diskretes Blau. Unter Wasser oder bei Regen aber verwandeln sie sich in lebendige Farbtupfer. Ansonsten gibt sich der Park beinahe monochrom. Dadurch lassen sich die Veränderungen besser erfahren, die die Zeit den Materialien zufügt. Denn schließlich, schreibt Georges Kubler, »sind die Formen der Zeit die Beute, die wir in Wirklichkeit fangen wollen«.

Jardin des Minoteries, Plainpalais, Geneva, Switzerland
Client: City of Geneva, Department for Urban Design and Public Lighting
(SAUEP)
Architect: Giordano Tironi in collaboration with Jean-Pierre Cêtre and
Jean-Marc Nusbaumer (engineers), Alfredo Mumenthaler (architect),
Alain Etienne (landscape architect responsible for the plantings)
Area: 5,400 square metres
Competition: 1995
Construction: 1996 – 1999

Berlin: Grafik auf Asphalt

Berlin: Drawing on asphalt

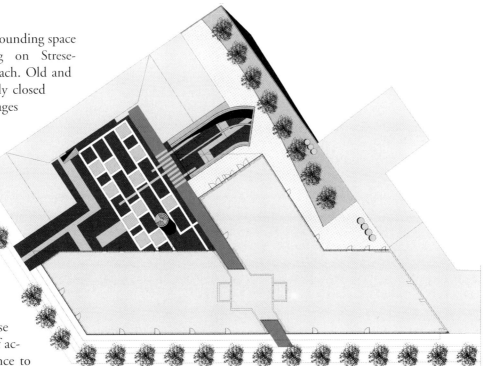

We wanted to develop the surrounding space of the administration building on Stresemannstrasse with a holistic approach. Old and modern buildings form a relatively closed ensemble in which the war damages still remain to be seen as historical breaches. The seven-storey modern building rises above the two-level underground garage which extends under the courtyard. The ground surface of the courtyard at the same time serves as the roof of the garage, and is thus part of the whole building. In this way a typical city area feature of multiple use is about to emerge, viz as a way of access to the building, as an entrance to the underground garage, as a loading zone for delivery vehicles and as an area of visual connection between old and modern buildings. The area makes an effect through its facade and ground surfaces. It was our aim to enhance the interaction between horizontal and vertical surfaces, different angles and broken lines in this location. We regard the ground surface in this project as a "fifth facade".

The ground surface is the area of contact between heaven and earth. It is the level at which most human activity takes place, and it is the source of all human creations. People paint, draw, structure and describe this area as if for someone who beholds it from above. The dialectical moment hinges upon the realisation that one's downward view always entails one's upward view.

Martin Rein-Cano
Lorenz Dexler

Die Außenanlagen des Versicherungsgebäudes an der Stresemannstraße wollten wir als ganzheitlichen Raum entwickeln. Alt- und Neubau bilden ein relativ geschlossenes Ensemble, in dem die Kriegsschäden als geschichtliche Brüche wahrnehmbar bleiben. Das sieben Stockwerke hohe neue Haus erhebt sich über einer zweigeschossigen Tiefgarage, die bis unter den Hof reicht. Die Bodenfläche des Hofes ist gleichzeitig Dach der Tiefgarage und Teil des gesamten Bauwerkes. Hier entsteht ein typischer Stadtraum mit mehrfacher Nutzung: als Zugang zum Gebäude, als Zufahrt zur Tiefgarage, als Vorfahrt für Lieferverkehr, als Verbindungshof zwischen Altbau und Neubau. Er wirkt durch seine Fassaden und Bodenflächen. Uns lag es daran, das Spiel von horizontalen und vertikalen Flächen, von unterschiedlichen Winkeln und gebrochenen Linien an diesem Ort zu verstärken. Wir betrachten den Boden als fünfte Fassade.

Als fünfte Fassade vermittelt der farbig gestaltete Hof des Bürogebäudes an der Stresemannstraße 111 zwischen Alt- und Neubau.

The colourfully designed courtyard of an administration building mediates like a "fifth facade" between old and modern buildings.

Kein roter Teppich, sondern ein Asphaltband weist Besuchern den Weg durch den Neubau über den Hof zum Altbau. Wo Autos auf der Fahrt in die Tiefgarage den Weg der Fußgänger kreuzen, löst sich ein Zebrastreifen-Motiv aus der abstrakten Grafik.

A band of concrete shows visitors the way through the new building across the courtyard to the old building. Where cars on their way to the underground garage cross the pedestrian path a zebra crossing motif unravels itself from the abstract graphic design.

" *The baroque form (...) is dynamic, aims at being vague in its effect (in its sway between fullness and emptiness, light and shade, broken lines and diverse angles of inclination), and suggests a progressive dissolution of space. The drive towards movement and illusion is responsible for the fact that the three-dimensional baroque masses never allow one to adopt any definitely preferred frontal perspective from which it could be viewed. It rather leads the beholder to constantly shift his point of perspective in order to perpetually see the object according to its new aspects as if it was involved in a process of continuous transformation.* "

Umberto Eco, The open work of art

Eine Fläche zu gestalten, heißt die Erdoberfläche zu formen. Hier berühren sich Himmel und Erde. Die Erdoberfläche ist die Ebene der menschlichen Bewegungen, der Ursprung des menschlichen Schaffens. Die Menschen bemalen, zeichnen, strukturieren und beschreiben diese Fläche wie für jemanden, der sie von oben betrachtet. Der dialektische Moment entsteht dadurch, dass der Blick nach unten immer den Blick nach oben be-

We find this kind of treatment of surfaces in many epochs of the history of mankind, like in the Neolithic age and among pre-Columbian cultures or also in the baroque. The surface not only served the people as an underlying surface for objects to be designed, but also as an object

Die Straßenverkehrsordnung stand Pate: Von den Straßen der Stadt bekannte Motive und Materialien fügen sich im Hof zu einem neuen Bild. Das Grundraster lieferte die Grafik der Neubaufassade. Um das Spiel der fluchtenden Linien und Ebenen zu verstärken, bemalten die Landschaftsarchitekten den Asphalt bis in die Tiefgarage hinein.

Authentic traffic signs inspired the design: Well-known motifs and materials from the city have been brought together to form a new design. The mural on the new building facade provided the basic pattern. In order to intensify the interplay of lines and planes of view the landscape architects painted the pavement all the way to the underground garage.

for design in its own right. White Horse and the gigantic Chalk Man in southern England, the large and inspiring figures in the high plains of Peru and the baroque broderie parterres in Europe are poignant examples. These help as points of reference for our project.

In order to develop the potential of the courtyard area we opted for asphalt as surface material and for the traffic sign colours of yellow, red and white. To use street drawings as an artistic element is part of the plan. We moulded the well-known materials, forms and colours prescribed by road traffic law into a new context where they

inhaltet. Einen solchen Umgang mit Flächen finden wir oft in der Geschichte der Menschheit – unter anderem im Neolithikum und in präkolumbischen Kulturen, oder auch im Barock. Die Fläche diente den Menschen dieser Kulturen nicht allein als Untergrund für zu gestaltende Objekte, sondern als Gestaltungsobjekt an sich. Bekannte Beispiele sind das »White Horse« und der gigantische »Chalk Man« im Süden Englands, die großen beflügelten Figuren in der peruanischen Hochebene und die barocken Broderie-Parterres in den Gartenanlagen europäischer Schlösser. Sie dienen uns als Referenz für unser Projekt.

Um die Kraft der Fläche im Hof des Verwaltungsgebäudes zu entfalten, entschieden wir uns für einen Untergrund aus dunklem Asphalt und Markierungsfarben in Gelb, Rot und Weiß. Straßengrafik als künstlerisches Element zu verwenden, ist Teil des Konzeptes. Die Materialien, Formen und

form their own abstract world of information. In order to emphasise the interaction between the surfaces and levels the painting extends into the underground garage. As a consequence different shifts in scales occur as well as mirroring fusions with the surrounding buildings.

Farben sind uns aus dem städtischen Raum bekannt, diktiert von der Straßenverkehrsordnung. In unserem Projekt stellten wir sie in einen neuen Kontext, wo sie eine eigene und abstrakte Informationswelt ergeben. Um das Spiel der Flächen und Ebenen zu betonen, zieht sich die Bemalung bis in die Tiefgarage hinein. Es entstehen Maßstabssprünge verschiedener Art sowie spiegelnde Verschmelzungen mit den umgebenden Gebäuden.

Free spaces of the Berlin branch of the DKV insurance company, Berlin
Client: Eigentümergenossenschaft Allianz-Lebensversicherungs AG/ DKV AG
Design: Topotek 1, Berlin
Architecture: Alsop & Störmer, Hamburg/ London
Size: 1,900 square metres
Planning: 1996 –1997
Construction: 1998 and 2000
Costs: DEM 450,000

Torrevieja: Holz für die Felsenküste

Torrevieja: Wood for a rocky coast

Carme Pinós

Durch unkontrolliertes Wachstum rückte die Küstenstadt Torrevieja in den vergangenen Jahrzehnten zu nahe ans Meer. Es blieb kaum mehr Raum für eine Strandpromenade oder für Badeplätze – ein Handikap für den zunehmenden Tourismus. Die Stadtverwaltung entschied deshalb, vor den Häuserfronten einen öffentlichen Raum am Wasser zu gestalten, der die vorhandenen knappen Flächen für Freizeit und Spiel möglichst geschickt ausnutzt und den vielen Menschen einen Zugang zum Meer bietet. Bisher erschwerten starke Wellen und schroffe Felsen das Baden erheblich. Als Architekten schlugen wir vor, durch den Ausbau zweier bestehender Molen den Raum zu erweitern und dabei zwei Buchten für Kinder zu schaffen, zum Baden und zum Spielen in der Sonne. Die Molen um-

Auf den schroffen Felsen vor dem Küstenort in Alicante schafft eine Promenade mit Holzpodesten Freiraum für Badegäste und Flaneure.

A promenade and wooden platforms create space for sunbathers and pedestrians along the jagged rocks of the coastal resort in Alicante.

Uncontrolled development has enabled the coastal town of Torrevieja to grow too close to the sea, leaving hardly any room for a waterside promenade or places to go swimming. For this reason, the town fathers decided to create public facilities along the water that would make skilful use of the restricted space while providing a place for recreation and games and access to the water. Since swimming was already difficult due to the heavy waves and jagged rocks, we suggested adapting two existing breakwaters to enlarge the amount of available space, thus creating two bays in which children can swim or play in the sun. The two breakwaters now enclose a play zone

Bestehende Wellenbrecher nutzen die Architekten, um zwei Badebuchten für Kinder einzurichten. Diagonal verlegtes, großformatiges Betonpflaster mit rautenförmigen Aussparungen für die Palmen verleiht der Promenade grafische Dynamik. Rampen, Sitz- und Liegepodeste bestehen aus Holz.

The existing breakwaters served the architects to create two bays for children to swim in. Diagonally arranged large-scale concrete tiles with lozenge-shaped gaps for palm trees lend a graphic kind of dynamics to the promenade. Ramps and pedestals for sitting and reclining on are made of wood.

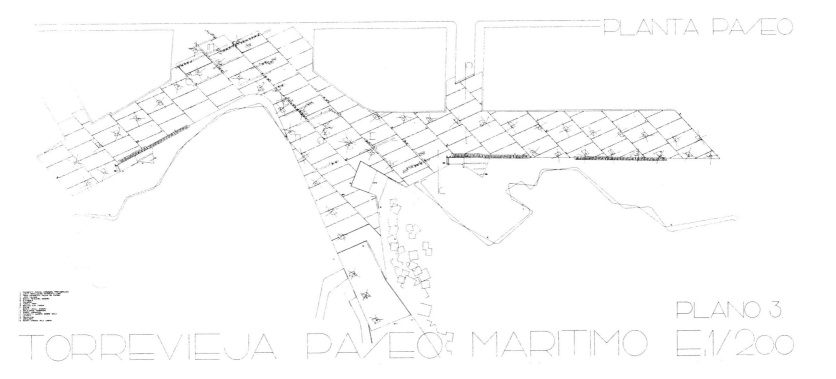

PLANTA PAVEO

PLANO 3.

TORREVIEJA PAVEO MARITIMO E.1/200

that contains swimming pools, wooden plat-forms and lighting fixtures, similar to the lines of a drawing submerged in water. We also created a waterside promenade and continued it out into the sea by providing the top of the breakwaters, which consist of huge concrete blocks, with a smooth level surface. This solution distributes people along the waterfront more effectively, and provides the town with a larger interface with the water. The waterfront is an attractive place for active occupations during the day, and suitable for more peaceful and contemplative strolling in the evening. When asked about the project, we like refer to the results as a coastal garden.

fassen nun eine Spielzone, in denen sich Badebecken, Leuchten und Holz-plattformen befinden. Von der Ferne und von den Häusern an der Wasser-front betrachtet, wirken diese Elemente sehr grafisch, wie eine Zeichnung im Wasser.

Über die bestehenden Molen führten wir die Uferpromenade gewisser-maßen ins Meer hinaus. Wir machten dadurch die riesigen, schwierig zu besteigenden Betonblöcke zugänglich, denen zuvor die Nähe zum Wasser vorbehalten war. Durch die Erweiterung des öffentlichen Raums verteilen sich die Spaziergänger und Badegäste nun weitläufig am Ufer, und die Stadt hat eine gestaltete Schwelle zum Meer erhalten. Tagsüber, so dachten wir uns, müsste die gesamte Wasserfront attraktiv sein für Spiel und Spaß, und in den Abendstunden sollte sie sich zum ruhigen, kontemplativen Ort für Flaneure wandeln. Wenn man uns fragt, erzählen wir gerne, dass wir hier einen »Meeresgarten« gebaut haben.

Waterside promenade Juan Aparicio, Torrevieja, Spain
Client: Torrevieja Town Council
Design: Carme Pinós, architect, with Juan Antonio Andreu, Javier Oliver,
Patricia Juncosa
Size: 7,000 square metres
Planning: 1996
Construction: 1999

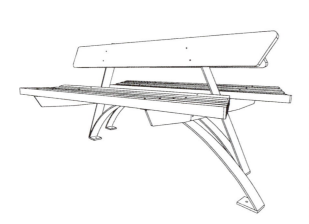

Wie zufällig verstreut wirken die flachen Holzbänke in Torrevieja. Extravagant geben sich hingegen die Bänke mit abgeschrägten Rückenlehnen und geschwungenen Metallfüßen. Palmen und schlichte Leuchten setzen einen Filter vor die Gebäude am Ufer.

The low wooden benches look scattered at random across the promenade in Torrevieja. Extravagant in comparison are the benches with slanting backs and curving metal legs. Palm trees and plain lamps form a filter in front of the shoreline buildings.

Stockholm: Recycling von Natur und Geschichte

Stockholm: Re-using nature and history

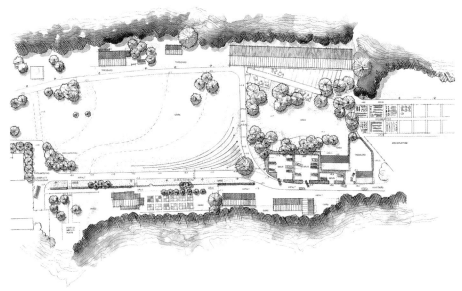

There was another one of those programmes about Japanese gardens on Swedish TV a few weeks ago. Besides presenting a number of rock gardens, it showed the famous moss garden in Kyoto, Saiho-ji. The camera traced the soft, undulating terrain covered with moss, punctuated only by bare tree trunks. A little stream cut through the grounds, which looked like layers of bedclothes. Light filtered down through semi-transparent canopies, the moving leaves creating a shifting play of light and shadow over the rolling surfaces with their various shades of green.

Saiho-ji, like all Zen gardens perhaps, is an exercise in reduction, in subtracting down to a level that consists of only three or four materials and five or six basic forms. Nevertheless, Saiho-ji is different from most Zen gardens. While they are abstractions, unnatural and constructed, Saiho-ji is apparently a piece of nature.

I have seen similar places in the Swedish countryside, where thin layers of soil, long winters and low temperatures create austere landscapes of distilled beauty. The harsh climate holds back the richness of nature. The difference between Saiho-ji and these landscapes is that there is no fence around the latter. If Zen monks came across such sites they could have their temple gardens ready made, merely by putting up a bamboo fence. Perhaps that would be the ultimate form of re-use: to re-use nature itself without exploiting it.

One such naturally beautiful place is Vinterviken, south of Stockholm. Its name means Winter Bay and refers to an old wintertime transportation route that once crossed the frozen waters of Lake Mälaren by sled, went up through the valley and continued on to Stockholm.

Vor einigen Wochen strahlte das schwedische Fernsehen wieder einmal einen Beitrag über japanische Gartenkunst aus. Er stellte neben einigen Steingärten auch den berühmten Moos-Garten in Kyoto, Saiho-ji, vor: eine sanfte, wellenförmige Moos-Landschaft, akzentuiert nur von einigen schlanken Baumstämmen. Ein kleiner Fluss hat seinen Weg durch die Landschaft wie durch einen Stapel Laken geschnitten und enthüllt die verschiedenen Bodenschichten. Das Licht scheint sanft durch das halbtransparente Blätterdach, und die im Wind tanzenden Blätter zeichnen Muster aus Licht und Schatten auf die wogenden, hell- und dunkelgrünen Hügel.

Saiho-ji ist, wie möglicherweise alle japanischen Zen-Gärten, ein Paradebeispiel für die Reduktion von Materialien und Formen. Sie geht soweit, dass am Ende nur noch drei oder vier verschiedene Materialien und fünf oder sechs Grundformen vorhanden sind. Und dennoch ist Saiho-ji anders als die meisten Zen-Gärten, die letztendlich doch nur Abstraktionen sind, unnatürlich und konstruiert. Saiho-ji erscheint im Gegensatz zu ihnen als ein Stück Natur.

In Schweden gibt es ähnliche Orte. Dünne Bodenschichten, lange Winter und niedrige Temperaturen haben dort schmucklose und karge Landschaften von reduzierter Schönheit geschaffen. Das raue Klima geizt hier mit dem Reichtum der Natur. Die schwedischen Landschaften unterscheiden sich allerdings vom Saiho-ji-Garten: Sie sind nicht von einem Zaun umgeben. Wären Zen-Mönche hier vorbeigekommen, sie hätten ihre Tempelgärten als Ready-made vorgefunden und bloß einen

Thorbjörn Andersson

Wie in japanischen Zen-Gärten ging es bei der Gestaltung des Freizeitparks Vinterviken darum, Materialien und Formen zu reduzieren.

As in Japanese Zen gardens, the design of the Vinterviken recreational park is about reduction in forms and materials.

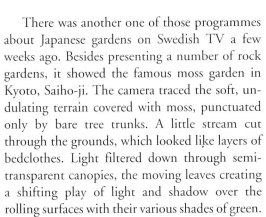

Vinterviken, ein ebenso idyllischer wie geschichtsträchtiger Ort, war den meisten Stockholmern bislang unbekannt. Das Büro FFNS gestaltete hier im Auftrag der Stadt einen Freizeitpark mit reduzierten Materialien und Formen. Den Mittelpunkt bildet eine offene Wiese, in der ehemaligen Fabrik befindet sich das Haus der Skulpturen.

Vinterviken, a place as idyllic as it is heavy with historic significance, was unknown to most Stockholmers until recently. The FFNS office, commissioned by the city, designed a recreational park with limited materials and forms on this site. The focus is on an open meadow; the former factory contains the Sculpture House.

Bambuszaun aufstellen müssen. So einen Garten zu schaffen, käme dem ultimativen Recycling nahe: die Natur selbst wiederverwerten, ohne sie auszubeuten. Vinterviken ist solch ein Ort, südlich von Stockholm gelegen. Der Name bedeutet Winterbucht und bezieht sich auf einen alten Transportweg, der im Winter genutzt wurde, als es kalt genug war, um mit dem Schlitten über den zugefrorenen Mälarsee bis nach Stockholm zu gelangen. Das Vinterviken-Tal ist zunächst flach, schneidet sich dann aber immer stärker ins Gelände. Wald bedeckt die steilen Talhänge, der Talgrund ist offen. An der Mündung, wo Fluss und See aufeinander treffen, weitet sich das Tal zu einer Graswiese auf. Diese ist von einer unbeschreiblichen natürli-

Vinterviken valley is shallow at the beginning and gradually deepens. The forest clings to its steep sides but the valley floor was kept open. It widens to a grassy meadow where the mouth of the valley meets the lake inlet. Despite its great natural beauty, the valley was unknown to most Stockholmers and seldom visited. It is tucked-away, secluded and secret. Yet Vinterviken was once a distinguished place. Alfred Nobel had his factories built on this site, where he had found a

Vor dem Haus der Skulpturen wurde ein dreieckiger Platz angelegt. Die Landschaftsarchitekten verwendeten hier recyceltes Pflaster und gusseiserne Platten. Die Skulptur stammt von Takashi Naraha.

A triangular square was set up in front of the Sculpture House. The landscape architects covered it with recycled granite cobblestones and cast iron flags. The sculpture is by Takashi Naraha.

safe repository for the sensitive and explosive nitro-glycerine. The steep sides of the valley could serve as protection against accidental explosions during handling. Nowadays, black limousines arrive in this abandoned valley every December, delivering Nobel Prize winners who pay their respects to the man who founded the prize. They do so by the memorial plaque on one of the hillsides. Such was the situation until the City of Stockholm voted to bring this hidden asset back to the attention of the Stockholmers. Vinterviken was to be made into a major recreational park for the south of the city. The project turned out to be one in which it was more important to subtract than to add. The heart of the project is the open meadow where the valley meets the lake inlet. To one side is the abandoned nitro-glycerine factory. Built of red brick, it is now a listed monument. It was turned into the Skulpturens Hus (House of Sculpture), an exhibition hall that presents a variety of Swedish and international sculptures. Our design intends to let the sculptures wander out of the building and eventually range throughout the valley. A triangular sculpture plaza was laid out in front of the factory. It is a plain hard surface surrounded by birches. The materials used are recycled granite cobblestones from the streets of Stockholm in combination with cast iron flags with a structured surface, originally meant as guidance markers for the blind.

The dirt road, which used to cut diagonally through the meadow, was shifted up over to one side. The meadow, thus uninterrupted, was sculpted into a shallow bowl and edged by a fan-shaped set of terrain steps to emphasise its rounded shape. One major objective was to attract people to discover the valley. In order to improve ac-

chen Schönheit, und dennoch bei den meisten Stockholmern unbekannt. So ist Vinterviken ein versteckter Platz, abgeschieden und geheim.

Blickt man in die Vergangenheit zurück, so war Vinterviken einmal ein ruhmreicher Ort. Alfred Nobel baute hier eine kleine Fabrik; die steilen Talhänge boten hervorragenden Schutz bei den Explosionsunfällen, die beim Umgang mit Nitroglycerin sehr oft passierten. Die Stadt Stockholm entschloss sich, diesen Ort in das Bewusstsein der Stockholmer zurück zu rufen. Vinterviken sollte in einen bedeutenden Freizeitpark für den südlichen Bereich der Stadt umgestaltet werden. Sehr rasch zeigte sich, dass es ein Projekt werden sollte, bei dem es mehr von Bedeutung war Dinge auszuschließen als hinzuzufügen.

Ein wesentliches Element des Projektes ist die offene Wiese an der Mündung von Fluss und See. Hier befinden sich die Überreste der ehemaligen, aus Ziegeln gebauten Nitroglycerinfabrik, die heute als Baudenkmal geschützt ist. Sie beherbergt jetzt das sogenannte Skulpturens Hus (Haus der Skulpturen), ein Ausstellungsgebäude, dass neben schwedischer Bildhauerkunst auch internationale Skulpturen zeigt. Im Rahmen des Projektes entstand die Idee, die Skulpturen auch außerhalb auszustellen. Hierzu wurde vor der Fabrik ein dreieckiger Skulpturenplatz angelegt. Er besteht aus

Fächerförmige Granitstufen strukturieren die Wiese vor dem Ausstellungsgebäude. Entlang des Kiesweges laden Bänke zum Verweilen ein. Die sechs Meter langen Einzelbänke können miteinander kombiniert werden.

Fan-shaped granite steps structure the meadow in front of the exhibition hall. Benches along the gravel path invite pedestrians to linger. Six metres in length, the benches can be joined together to form larger units.

Vinterviken lässt sich vom Stadtzentrum aus mit Fähr-schiffen bequem erreichen. Ein Sonnendeck aus Lärchenholz erwartet die Besucher am Bootssteg.
Vinterviken is easy to reach by ferry from the city centre. A larchen sundeck awaits visitors by the dock.

einer einfachen harten Oberfläche und ist von Birken umgeben. Das Material stammt aus den Straßen Stockholms: recycelter Granit, der in Kombination mit gusseisernen Platten mit Struktur-Oberfläche aufgebracht wurde, die ursprünglich Blinden zur Orientierung dienen sollte. Wichtig war auch, die Bevölkerung dazu zu bringen, Vinterviken neu zu entdecken. Um den Zugang zu erleichtern, wurde eine Fährverbindung eingerichtet und eine Bootsanlegestelle gebaut – ein großes Sonnendeck aus Lärchenholz, das die ankommenden Schiffe begrüßt.

Im Rahmen des Projektes wurden einige ausgewählte Objekte gestaltet, die als Wahrzeichen dem Ort Charakter geben sollen, beispielsweise ein Laternenpfahl, der in seiner Form und Gestalt an alte Industrielampen erinnert. Entlang des neuen Kiesweges durch das Tal stehen nun mehrere große Bänke, jeweils sechs Meter lang und kombinierbar zu einer zwölf Meter langen Konstruktion. So können sie auch ganzen Familien als Picknickplätze dienen. Trotz dieser Ergänzungen achteten wir bei der Planung darauf, dass mehr reduziert als hinzugefügt wurde. Unterhalb einer Autobahnbrücke entfernten wir das dichte Gestrüpp und schufen so auf dem nackten Fels zwischen den Betonstützen der Brücke einen Raum, der einer Kathedrale ähnelt. Hier liegt nun der Parkplatz.

Die Waldränder wurden ausgedünnt, um den Pflanzengesellschaften des Waldsaumes einen Lebensraum zu bieten. Einige Eichen erhielten mehr Platz, Fichten wurden entfernt, Haselnuss und Eberesche kamen hinzu. Wir befreiten den Boden von Sämlingen und Strauchunterwuchs, um die Ansiedlung von Kräutern wie Buschwindröschen (Anemone nemorosa), Wiesenschlüsselblume (Primula veris) oder Maiglöckchen (Convallaria majalis) zu ermöglichen. Am Rande des Flusses rissen wir beinahe 90 Prozent der dichten Ufervegetation weg, da sie nicht nur den Blick auf das Tal, sondern auch den Zugang zum Wasser verhinderte. Heute steht hier eine transparente Wand aus Erlen und Weiden, die durch ihr Blätterdach hindurch einladen, den Blick über die kleine Bucht streifen zu lassen, die einst dem Tal seinen Namen gab.

Vinterviken recreational park, south of Stockholm, Sweden
Landscape architect: Thorbjörn Andersson (head), Anders Lidström, Clotte Frank
and Johan Paju of FFNS Architects, Stockholm
Size: 50,000 square metres
Planning: 1996 – 1998
Construction: 1998 – 1999
Costs: SEK 24 million

cess, a ferry boat line was established that lands here. The landing itself received special attention as the all-important point of arrival. A broad sundeck made of larch complements the dock and provides space for sun-worshippers.

A selection of objects was designed as distinctive hard emblems that create focal points to lend character to the valley. One of these is a lamppost inspired by old industrial lamps and steel pole structures. Another is a large-scale bench, which is positioned at intervals along the new gravel path that leads along the valley floor. Six metres long, these benches can be linked to form a 12-metre structure that can be used for seating, as a platform for a family picnic, or for stretching out in the sun. All in all, however, more was taken away than was added. The area under the motorway bridge that crosses the valley was cleared of dense vegetation, exposing the blasted rock walls and creating a cathedral-like space among the concrete columns. This is where the parking lot was placed in order to prevent traffic further down the valley.

The edges of the forest were thinned out to encourage the development of the most characteristic plants. Certain oak trees were given more room; all spruce was removed; hazel and mountain ash were favoured. The ground was cleared of seed-bred shrubs and shoots to promote spontaneous colonisation by herbs such as *Anemone nemorosa, Primula veris, Convallaria majalis.* Along the shore of the inlet, close to 90 per cent of the dense lakeside vegetation that prevented visual as well as physical contact with the water was cleared away. Now there is a thin screen of alders and willows inviting views of the lake inlet that gave the valley its name.

Jordbro: Kiefern im Corten-Stahl-Rahmen

Jordbro: Pine trees within a Cor-Ten steel surround

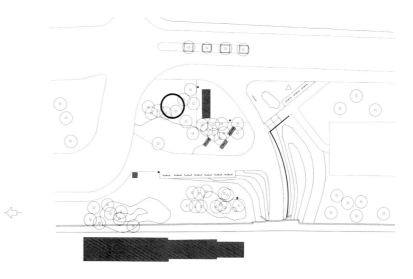

In December 1997, the community of Haninge invited me and a colleague, the sculptor Hans Peterson, to draw up a proposal for a project concerned with refurbishing the precinct at Jordbro railway station. Since one percent of the communal budget is invested in art, the aim was also to find a new form for art in public spaces. The project thus provided us with an opportunity to thoroughly investigate the relationship between art and landscape architecture, and thus determine whether art can be an integral part of public space. Jordbro is a district of Haninge, and is located 30 kilometres south of the centre of Stockholm. Although the home of two generations of Haninge citizens, 35 percent of Jordbro's inhabitants are of a foreign background, and with its sixties-style housing it makes the impression of a typical underprivileged suburb. The precinct at the railway station connects a bus terminal and a car park, whereby a main pedestrian pathway passes the station park and continues on to the local commercial district. Before the alteration measures, the precinct had a negative identity determined by a pedestrian tunnel leading to the rail platforms, and a steep pathway leading up to

Im Dezember 1997 gab die Stadt Haninge meinem Kollegen, dem Bildhauer Hans Peterson, und mir den Auftrag für die Neugestaltung des Umfeldes am Bahnhof von Jordbro. Da ein Prozent des kommunalen Haushalts für Kunst bereitgestellt wird, wollte man eine neue Form von Kunst im öffentlichen Raum finden. Jordbro, ein aus den 60er Jahren stammender Stadtteil von Haninge, liegt 30 Kilometer südlich der Innenstadt von Stockholm. Seit zwei Generationen leben die Menschen hier, 35 Prozent der Einwohner sind ausländischer Herkunft, und viele sind arbeitslos. Das Bahnhofsumfeld von Jordbro besteht aus einem Busbahnhof und dem Parkplatz. Über ihn verläuft ein wichtiger Fußweg zum örtlichen Einkaufszentrum. Vor der Umgestaltung hatte der Ort einen üblen Ruf – dazu trug vor allem die Fußgängerunterführung zu den Bahnsteigen bei, und der steile Fußweg, der vom Parkplatz schier verschluckt wurde. Die meisten Bewohner sind Pendler und passieren zweimal täglich diesen Ort beim Wegfahren und Wiederkommen. Kein grandioser Eindruck bot sich ihnen bisher: ein gewöhnlicher anonymer, charakterloser Platz. Wir machten es uns zum Ziel, einen Platz mit eigener Note zu gestalten und ihn in seine Umgebung zu integrieren. Eine städtebauliche Analyse zeigte seine klare räumliche Struktur bestehend aus drei parallelen, linearen Elementen: der Bahnlinie, der Hauptstraße und den drei bis fünf geschossigen Mietshäusern, die um grüne Innenhöfe herum gruppiert sind. Den lichten, alten Kiefernwald nahmen wir als identitätsstiftenden Blickpunkt.

Jonas Berglund

Bodenwellen und eine Stahlskulptur machen den Bahnhofsvorplatz des Stockholmer Vorortes zum Blickfang für Pendler.

Sinuous ground modelling and a steel sculpture make the station precinct at a Stockholm suburb an attractive sight for commuters.

Schlichtheit als Leitmotiv: Ein Corten-Stahl-Ring rahmt vier Kiefern – und erinnert damit an die zahlreichen Wälder dieser Gegend. Sanftes Licht in den U-Profilen des Ringes taucht den neu gestalteten Bahnhofsvorplatz bei Nacht in ein geheimnisvolles Licht.

Simplicity as a leitmotiv: a Cor-Ten steel ring frames four pines, thus recalling the many forests in the region. The soft light in the U-shaped profile of the ring plunges the newly designed square in front of the railway station into mysterious light at night.

Aus der Analyse ergab sich das Konzept für die Neugestaltung. Wir arbeiteten mit einem Sandmodell im Maßstab 1:100 und modellierten den Fußgängerweg, um den Bahnhof mit der Hauptstraße zu verbinden. Ein skulpturaler Corten-Stahl-Ring und eine wellenförmige Erdmodellierung akzentuieren den Platz und machen alle anderen zeichenhaften Elemente unnötig. Während der Arbeit am Modell kamen Erinnerungen an einen längst vergessenen Park aus dem 19. Jahrhundert hoch, der sich einst an dieser Stelle befunden hatte. Der Corten-Stahl-Ring und die Bänke aus Beton und Eichenholz nehmen Bezug auf ihn. Der Ring mit seinem Radius

and overpowered by the parking area. Passed through twice a day by most inhabitants, the precinct was nondescript and anonymous. Our aim was to form a clearly defined space with a character that had to be a genuine part of the place. The railway station and the commercial district are the most important components of the suburban structure. Considering this fact, we sought to give the important but neglected precinct a distinct form. To do this, we made an urban analysis to define the functions, flow and character of the spatial situation. This revealed the station as being the most important node in Jordbro, a place that commuters pass through in twice-daily flows. The analysis also demonstrated a clear urban structure, consisting of three parallel elements: the railway, the main street, and three-to-five-storey social housing grouped around green yards. Pine trees (*Pinus silvestris*) lend the area character and create visual links.

The analysis provided us with the inspiration for our proposal, and our next step was to create a sand model on a scale of 1:100 in which we clearly defined the main pedestrian route to link the station to the main street. The route is emphasised by sculptural Cor-Ten steel and sinuous earth modelling, thus reducing the need for signs while also creating identity. It was while we were working on the model that we recalled the forgotten 19th-century station park. This provided us with a typological tool to which we added two elements: a circular Cor-Ten steel sculpture, and three oak and concrete benches. The circle provides the park with a focal point while also taking up the theme of the sinuous pathway. Measuring 4.5 meters in circumference, it encloses four pine trees to recall the beauty of the forests that once grew profusely in the area. We reduced the use of materials to simple, low-budget elements with no associative meaning, such as grass, tarmac and Cor-Ten steel, in order to strengthen the formal concept. In order to also give the area a distinct character at night, the circle has been given soft lighting integrated in its U-shaped profile. The rest of the lighting consists of spotlights on a single mast hidden among the pine trees.

Den einst anonymen Bahn-hofsvorplatz verwandelten der Künstler Hans Peterson und der Landschaftsarchitekt Jonas Berglund in einen künstlerischen Ort, den zwei starke Zeichen prägen, eine Stahlskulptur und Bodenwellen. Bänke aus Beton und Eiche erinnern an einen längst vergessenen Park, der sich hier einst befand. Bei der Einweihung des Platzes im Mai nutzten Schauspieler der Gruppe Tiger den Platz als Kulisse.

The artist Hans Peterson and the landscape architect Jonas Berglund transformed an undistinguished square in front of a railway station into an artistic site. Two bold elements stand out: a steel sculpture and undulating ground. Benches made of concrete and oak recall a long-forgotten park that used to be here. When the square was inaugurated this May, the Tiger troupe's actors used it as a stage set.

von 4,50 Metern soll den Mittelpunkt des Parks bilden und den Schwung des Fußgängerweges aufnehmen. Er umfasst vier Kiefern und setzt damit der Schönheit der einstmals üppigen Wälder dieser Gegend ein Zeichen. Wir haben einfache, kostengünstige Materialien verwendet: Rasen, Asphalt und Corten-Stahl. Ohne irgendwelche Anspielungen wollten wir Schlichtheit bis ins letzte Detail herstellen. Um dem Platz schließlich ein Gesicht bei Nacht zu geben, integrierten wir sanftes Licht in die U-Profile des Ringes. Ansonsten reicht es aus, den Platz von Spots an einem einzigen Mast aus zu beleuchten, der sich zwischen den Stämmen der Kiefern verbirgt.

Jordbro Station Park, Haninge near Stockholm, Sweden
Client: City of Haninge, Technical Service (Petra Lindvall), Cultural Department (Elisabeth Åström)
Design: Jonas Berglund, landscape architect at Stockholm Konsult, Hans Peterson, landscape architect and artist,
and Helena Björnberg, lighting engineer
Size: 5,000 square metres
Competition: 1997
Planning: 1998
Construction: 1999
Costs: SEK 1.5 million (including SEK 395,000 for art work)

Berlin: die Botschaften der nordischen Länder

Berlin: The Nordic embassy complex

Alfred Berger
Tiina Parkkinen

Kupfer, Wasser und Licht prägen das nordische Botschaftsviertel und signalisieren Individualität wie Gemeinsamkeit.

The design elements of copper, water and light signalise both individuality and communality of purpose at an embassy compound in Berlin.

Die fünf nordischen Länder Dänemark, Finnland, Island, Norwegen und Schweden errichteten ihre diplomatischen Vertretungen in Berlin, der langen Tradition ihrer Zusammenarbeit entsprechend, auf einem gemeinsamen Grundstück – ergänzt von einem Gemeinschaftsgebäude und gerahmt von einem 226 Meter langen und 15 Meter hohen Kupferband.

Das Band. In seiner fließenden, kontinuierlichen Bewegung verwandelt das Band den Botschaftskomplex in eine kompakte Landmarke im Herzen Berlins. 3850 grün patinierte Kupferlamellen sorgen dabei für ein spannungsreiches Verhältnis zwischen Innen und Außen. Die Kupferelemente mit unterschiedlichen Neigungswinkeln rhythmisieren das Band und lassen das Innere nach Außen scheinen. An der Rauchstraße öffnet sich das Band an der Stelle, von der aus das Gelände erschlossen wird: Von hier aus lässt sich das raffinierte Zusammenspiel der Botschaften überblicken.

Das Grün. Eine Rasenfläche rahmt das Kupferband außen, bestanden von einzelnen Bäumen. Ein umlaufendes, etwa zehn Zentimeter hohes Edelstahlband markiert die Grenze zum

In continuation of a long tradition of close collaboration, the five Nordic countries of Denmark, Finland, Iceland, Norway and Sweden have set up their embassies in Berlin on a joint piece of property surrounded by a copper band 226 metres long and 15 metres high. Also included is a building for joint use.

The copper band. In its continuous flowing movement, the copper band transforms the embassy compound into a compact landmark in the heart of Berlin. Some 3,850 copper slats with a verdigris patina create interesting relationships between inside and outside. Moreover, being tipped at various angles, they introduce a feeling of rhythm while also allowing occasional glimpses of the inside. The band opens at the entrance at Rauch Strasse, from where a good idea can be gained of the way in which the embassies interact.

The green elements. An area of lawn with individual trees flanks the outside of the enclosure, and is faced by a 10-centimetre-high stainless steel band that marks the boundary to the streetspace. The existing stock of elm and poplar trees has been supplemented with birches (*Betula pendula 'tristis'*) to emphasise the Nordic character of the site. The black and white bark and the dense, bright green foliage of the trees form an initial filter between the streetspace and the copper band, thus emphasising the transition from nature (the complex is located at Tiergarten) to architecture.

The plaza. The embassy buildings are centred around a plaza. The simple, semi-public area adapts easily to differing uses, ranging from normal everyday activities to festive ceremonies. Narrow strips of white Ekeberg marble from Sweden featuring ground lights repeat the main

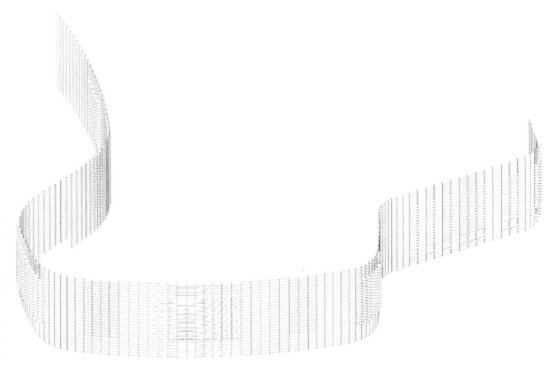

geometrical lines of the site and underscore the spatial perspective of the buildings. Otherwise the paving consists of unfinished rust-brown Norwegian quartz slate (Otter Phylilit Colorit), and wood-block larch below the entrance canopy.

The water basin. In reminiscence of the sea, which surrounds all Nordic countries, a water basin with a clear geometric shape transects the compound and continues on to outside the copper band, which is cut away above the water to provide passers-by with views of the inside. The water basin lies between the five main buildings like an elegant vessel, and thus reflects them all, and its white coloration awakens associations with the Northern spring, when the ice begins to crack and melt.

The canopy. A canopy made of Teflon-coated glass-fibre fabric divides the compound into an inner and outer area and covers both the entrance zone and the ramp leading down to the underground garage. It hovers above this transition area like a flying object, and in connection with the security fence forms a kind of loggia for waiting or arriving guests. At night, luminous elements incorporated into the fabric transform the roof into a cloud of light. The fabric membranes are borne by a structural framework supported by parabolic arches and made of laminated wood and stainless steel.

The lighting. The lighting concept refers to the special characteristics of Nordic light. Instead of installing lighting fixtures or illuminating the buildings from the outside like old churches, light shines through the semi-glazed facades and illuminates the open spaces. Punctuated ground lights underscore the geometry of the plaza and

öffentlichen Straßenraum. Der vorhandene Baumbestand aus Ulmen und Pappeln wurde durch Hänge-Birken (Betula pendula 'tristis') ergänzt, um den nördlichen Charakter der Anlage zu betonen. Die schwarzweißen Birkenstämme mit ihrem nicht zu dichten lichtgrünen Laub bilden den ersten Filter vor dem Kupferband und erhöhen die Spannung von Natur zur Architektur.

Die Plaza. Das Herzstück der Anlage bildet die Plaza. Der schlichte, halböffentliche Platz passt sich seiner jeweiligen Nutzung an, sei es an gewöhnlichen Arbeitstagen oder zu festlichen Empfängen. Schmale, weiße Streifen schwedischen Marmors (Ekeberg-Marmor) mit eingebauten Bodenleuchten zeichnen im Pflaster aus rostbraunem, spaltrauhem Quarzschiefer aus Norwegen (Otter Phylilit Colorit) die geometrischen Leitlinien des Entwurfs nach und verstärken so die räumliche Perspektive der Baukörper. Ein Holzbohlenbelag aus Lärchenholz markiert den Eingang, die Schwelle zwischen Stadt und Botschaften.

Das Wasserbecken. Als Erinnerung an das Meer, das alle nordischen Länder umgibt, durchschneidet ein Wasserbecken in klarer geometrischer Form die Anlage und durchstößt das Kupferband beidseitig. Wie ein elegantes Gefäß liegt es zwischen den fünf Gebäuden. Die fast weiße Färbung des Bassins erweckt Assoziationen an ein Meer im Frühling, wenn das Eis Risse bekommt und etwas Wasser auf seine Oberfläche dringt. Alle fünf Botschaften spiegeln sich im Wasser. Das Kupferband ist über dem Wasserspiegel leicht ausgeschnitten und gestattet somit Passanten Einblicke in die Anlagen.

Das Flugdach. Ein Dach teilt die Anlage in einen inneren und einen äußeren Bereich und überspannt die Eingangszone sowie die Tiefgaragenrampe. Das dynamisch geformte Volumen des Textilkörpers schwebt wie

Den Empfangsbereich überspannt ein textiles Flugdach. Rechts das Gemeinschaftshaus Felleshuset, dahinter die Finnische und die Norwegische Botschaft, links Dänemark. Alle Gebäude sind eingepasst in ein fließendes Kupferband. Die Logik des Entwurfs: das Kupferband, die Baukörper, die Leerräume, die Schnittlinien, die Gebäudemasse, das Grundstück.

A suspended fabric canopy spans the entrance area. On the right is the Felleshus building for joint use, behind it are the Finnish and Norwegian embassies, and on the left is the Danish one. All buildings are surrounded by a flowing copper band. The logic of the design: the copper band, the buildings, the empty spaces, the intersecting lines, the buildings' total volume, the lot.

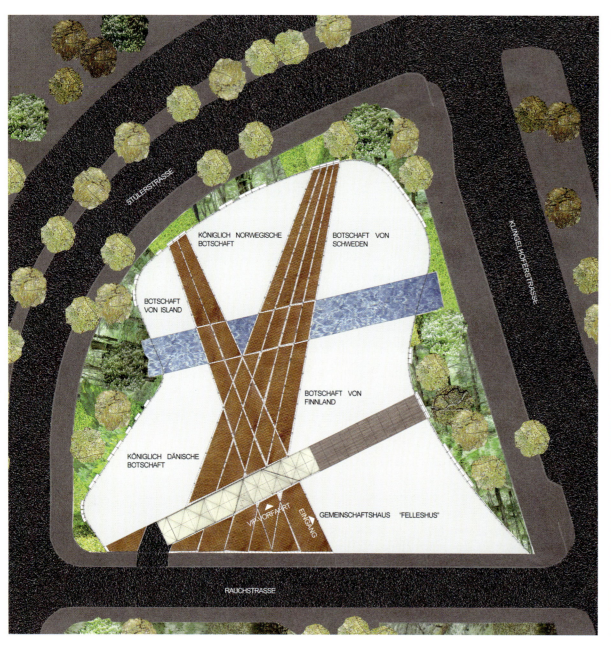

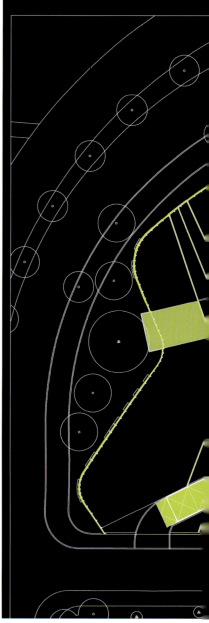

The Embassies of the Nordic Countries in Berlin
Client: Statens Fastighetsverk, Stockholm
Architects: Berger + Parkkinen, Vienna (Alfred Berger and Tiina Parkkinen with Margarete Dietrich, Antti Laiho, Ines Nicic, Thomas Pirker, Kurt Sattler, Peter Thalbauer, Günther Unterfrauner, and Ivan Zdenkovic) for the master plan, joint building, basement, copper band, outdoor facilities, canopy, and urban development co-ordination
Size: 7,290 square metres
Competition: 1995
Completion: 1999
Costs: DEM 97 million

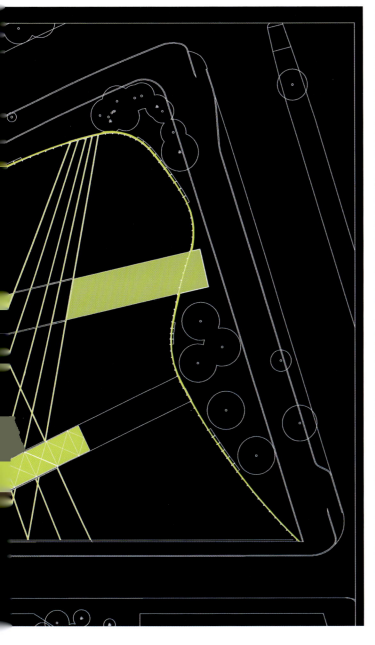

Schmale Schneisen mit starkem Licht- und Schattenspiel bestechen im Raum- und Beleuchtungskonzept der Architekten Berger + Parkkinen. Die Gebäude werden nicht angestrahlt, sie leuchten vielmehr von innen heraus. Vertikales Licht betont die gewölbten Kupferelemente des Bandes; Leuchtpunkte im Boden betonen das Herzstück der Anlage, die Plaza.

Narrow lanes with powerfully contrasting light and shade feature in the spatial and lighting concepts of Berger + Parkkinen architects. The buildings are not floodlit, but glow from within instead. Vertical light brings out the convex elements on the copper band; point lighting in the ground underscores the heart of the project: the plaza.

ein Flugobjekt über dieser Schwelle und bildet gemeinsam mit dem Sicherheitszaun eine Art Loggia für wartende oder ankommende Gäste. Nachts verwandeln im Inneren des Textilkörpers angebrachte Leuchtkörper das Dach in eine leuchtende Wolke. Ein Rahmenfachwerk aus Leimschichtholz und Edelstahl mit parabelförmigen Druckbögen trägt die Textilmembranen. Sie bestehen aus teflonbeschichtetem Glasfasergewebe.

Das Licht. Das Beleuchtungskonzept nimmt Bezug auf die Besonderheit des nordischen Lichts. Anstatt Leuchtkörper aufzustellen, werden die vorhandenen Elemente der Anlage zu Leuchten. Die Botschaftsgebäude werden nicht angestrahlt wie alte Steinkirchen, sondern sie leuchten selbst. Das Licht dringt aus dem Inneren der Gebäude durch die leichten Fassaden und erhellt den öffentlichen Raum. Eine Reihe von Leuchtpunkten im Boden betont die Geometrie des Platzraumes. Sie sind entlang der Anlage plaziert und ermöglichen die Orientierung auch bei stark reduziertem Allgemeinlicht. Über dem Eingang taucht das Flugdach den Ankunftsbereich in sanftes Licht.

Das helle Wasserbecken bildet eine weitere Lichtquelle. Strahler in den Seitenwänden machen es zu einem fluoreszierenden, leicht wogenden Lichtkörper. Das so bewegte Licht projiziert ein tanzendes Netz auf die angrenzenden Fassaden. Der Außenbereich wird geprägt vom ständig wechselnden Bild der leuchtenden Gebäude und den hofartigen Räumen. Im Kontrast dazu steht die passive, gleichbleibende Leuchtkraft des Kupferbandes. Eine vertikal gerichtete Lichtstrahlung betont die Plastizität der gewölbten Kupferelemente. Wiederum wird das Bauteil für den Betrachter zur Lichtquelle, und die eigentlichen Leuchten bleiben für ihn verborgen.

facilitate orientation in conditions of reduced ambient light, and at night the canopy bathes the entrance area in a soft glow.

The white water basin is a further source of illumination. This is due to directional lights let into the side walls, making the basin a gently rocking luminous element that throws dancing patterns onto neighbouring facades. As the lights go on and off inside the embassy buildings, this results in changes in the luminosity of the buildings and thus of the court-like spaces outside. This effect is contrasted by the unchanging lit appearance of the copper band, in which vertical lighting emphasises the convex shape of the individual elements, and turns them into a further source of indirect illumination.

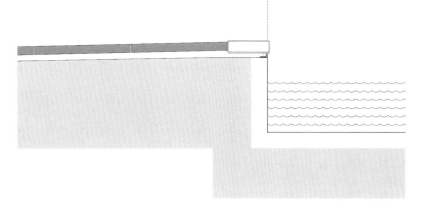

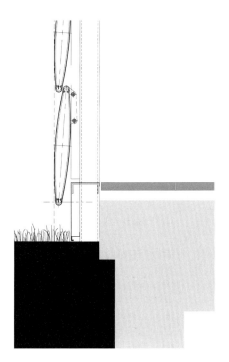

Auf der Plaza wurde weißer schwedischer Marmor und rostbrauner Quarzschiefer aus Norwegen verlegt. Detailzeichnung des Anschlusspunkts des Natursteinbelags an das Wasserbecken, daneben der Anschluss an das Kupferband.

The plaza was paved with white Swedish marble and rusty-brown Norwegian quartz slate. The detail drawing shows where the natural stone pavement meets the pool, and (on the right) where it meets the copper band.

Manchester: »Pudding-Stein« trifft Granit und Stahl

Manchester: "Pudding-stone" meets granite and steel

Exchange Square is a new civic plaza located in the heart of Manchester, England. It lies between the retail core of the City Centre and the Millennium Quarter. A roughly triangular area of 10,000 square metres, the plaza is bounded by shopping to the east and south, and by the Cathedral District to the north.

In 1996 an IRA bomb blast levelled this area of Manchester. The rebuilding of the centre became part of the greater "Millennium" initiative to rebuild areas of the country. It was envisioned that the rebuilding of this square would play an important role for the city, acting as a catalyst to re-energise the northern section of the city. The city planners conceived of Exchange Square as the focus of a series of improved streetscapes and major open spaces that would link the rebuilding initiatives of the renewal area.

Site. The complex site ties together such historically significant buildings as the Corn Exchange and the Shambles Pub with the brand new building of Mark's and Spencer's, besides connecting to the renovated Printworks and Arndale Centre. The north edge of the site is defined by the strong curve of the Corn Exchange Building and the grand arc of Hanging Ditch Road. This paved road was once a water flume, which branched off the Irk River into the Irwell. The arced water element came to form the boundary line between the old Cathedral District of the city and the newer shopping district. The great Cathedral, carved out of the existing "pudding stone" of the underlying bedrock, was bombed during World War II and rebuilt. Today, the grid of the newly built shopping district crashes into the medieval arc of the Cathedral District at Exchange Square. In addition, this shopping district

Der Exchange Square ist ein neuer öffentlicher Platz im Zentrum von Manchester, zwischen dem quirligen Zentrum und dem Millennium-Viertel gelegen. Die dreieckige Fläche von etwa 10 000 Quadratmetern wird im Osten und Süden von Geschäften begrenzt, im Norden trifft sie auf das Kathedralen-Viertel. 1996 legte eine Bombe der IRA diesen Stadtteil in Schutt und Asche. Im Rahmen der landesweiten »Millennium«-Initiative wurde er wieder aufgebaut. Dem Platz wurde große Bedeutung als eine Art Katalysator beigemessen, der den Norden der Stadt mit neuer Energie erfüllen und genügend Anziehungskraft ausüben sollte, um die Leute weg von den bereits belebten Stadtteilen hin zu neuen Angeboten im Millennium-Viertel zu locken. Die Stadtplaner sehen den Exchange Square als die Krönung mehrerer aufgewerteter Straßen und Freiflächen, welche die sanierten Areale miteinander verbinden.

Am Ort befinden sich historisch bedeutsame Gebäude wie die Getreidebörse und der Shambles Pub, außerdem das brandneue Gebäude des Kaufhauses Mark's and Spencer's. Den Nordrand definieren die markante Kurve der Getreidebörse und der eindrucksvolle Bogen der Hanging Ditch Road. Diese gepflasterte Straße war einst ein Kanal, der die Flüsse Irk und Irwell mit-

Martha Schwartz
Shauna Gillies-Smith

Spannungsvoll gestaltet, vermittelt der Exchange Square zwischen dem Cathedral District und dem industriell geprägten Manchester.

The exciting tension of Exchange Square forms the transition between the Cathedral District and industrial Manchester.

Ein volles Stockwerk trennt die beiden Platzhälften des Exchange Square voneinander. Die Landschaftsarchitekten überbrückten den Höhensprung mit geschwungenen Sitzmauern und Rampen. So entstand eine belebte Durchgangszone, die zugleich als Ort des Verweilens dient.

A difference in height of one full storey separates the two halves of Exchange Square. The landscape architects bridged the jump with curving ramps and walls with integrated seats. The result was a lively transit zone that also serves as a place to relax and linger.

Martha Schwartz, Inc.

approaches the square one full storey above the level of the Cathedral District. Here the shift in elevation becomes evident and must be resolved.

Concept. The concept of the design was generated through both the cultural and geological history of the site, and through the expression of the grade change that is fundamental to the site's character and use. The design and organisation of the site express the "seam," or line at which the two distinct parts of the city come together. The concept is about the stitching together of the two different fabrics of the city. The northern portion of the site, the Cathedral District, is built of yellowish "pudding stone," the material of the bluff upon which the Cathedral sits. It is a material which speaks of tradition and convention. This part of the plaza accommodates outdoor restaurants and bars. The new design of the plaza is characterised by a long, linear water feature that re-introduces the old "Hanging Ditch" to the site. This ditch must be crossed in order to access either side of the plaza. The upper plaza, or southern portion of the site, sits a full storey above the "Hanging Ditch." This part is built of granite, glass and steel. Paths that recall railway tracks run parallel across the upper plaza. Railway carriage benches sit on the rails. The railway imagery refers back to the inception of the Industrial Revolution in Manchester, where the development of the railway as a transport system was as responsible for the explosion of industrialisation as the manufacturing process itself. The materials and the orthogonal structure of the design mark this section as the "modern" Manchester.

The two areas, or "fabrics" of the site are knitted together along a strong, sculptural "seam" of serial ramps which link the lower plaza to the up-

einander verband. Der Kanalbogen wurde zur Grenzlinie zwischen dem Kathedralen-Viertel und der Einkaufszone. Die großartige Kathedrale, aus heimischem »Pudding-Stein« gemeißelt, war im zweiten Weltkrieg bombardiert und danach wieder aufgebaut worden. Heute stößt auf dem Exchange Square das Raster des jüngeren Geschäftsviertels unmittelbar auf den mittelalterlichen Bogen des Kathedralen-Viertels – ein volles Stockwerk trennt die beiden Viertel zudem voneinander. Dieser Höhenunterschied springt ins Auge und gab den Auftakt für unseren Entwurf.

Das Konzept. Gestaltung und Organisation des Ortes beziehen sich ausdrücklich auf jene Nahtstelle, an der die zwei unterschiedlichen Texturen der Innenstadt aufeinanderstoßen. Es geht darum, die zwei verschiedenartigen Stoffe zusammenzunähen. Der nördliche Teil des Platzes besteht aus demselben Tuffstein wie das Kathedralen-Viertel – der gelbliche »Puddingstein« versinnbildlicht damit Tradition und Konvention. Hier befinden sich Straßencafés und Restaurants. Blickpunkt der Neugestaltung ist ein langes, schmales Wasserbecken, das den alten Wassergraben, den »Hanging Ditch«, wieder auferstehen lassen soll. Auf dem Weg über den Platz muss man zwangsläufig diesen Wasserlauf überqueren.

Der obere, südliche Teil des Platzes liegt ein volles Stockwerk über dem »Hanging Ditch«. Hier dominieren Granit, Glas und Stahl. Parallele Wege, die an Bahngleise erinnern und auf denen waggonähnliche Bänke befestigt

Der gelbliche »Puddingstein«-Tuff des historischen Manchester kennzeichnet die untere Platzhälfte. Ein Wasserlauf zeichnet den alten »Hanging Ditch«-Graben nach. Dicht mit bündig geschnittenen Steinen aufgefüllt, lässt er sich einfach überqueren. Auf dem Granitpflaster des oberen Platzes stehen Stahlbänke mit echten Eisenbahnrädern und einer blauen Kunststoffsitzfläche.

The yellowish "pudding stone" tufa of historic Manchester characterises the lower half of the square. A linear water feature traces the original "Hanging Ditch." Closely filled up with stones trimmed flush with each other, it can easily be crossed. Standing on the granite paving of the upper square, the steel benches have genuine railway wheels and blue plastic seats.

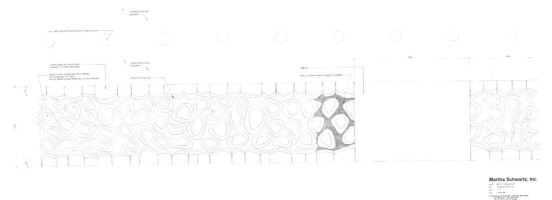

Martha Schwartz, Inc.

Auf dem Grund des »Hanging-Ditch«-Wasserlaufes befinden sich kleine Ventile zwischen den Steinen, die das Wasser nach oben spritzen und einen stürmischen Bach suggerieren. Holzpodeste wurden an drei Stellen bündig zum Pflaster über den Bach gelegt.

In the bed of the water feature in the "Hanging Ditch" small valves between the stones squirt water upwards and suggest a rushing brook. Wooden platforms flush with the paving were laid across the brook in three places.

wurden, laufen quer über den Platz. Das Eisenbahn-Motiv erinnert an den Beginn der industriellen Revolution in Manchester und daran, dass die Bahn als neues Transportmittel genauso Motor der Industrialisierung war wie die neuen Produktionstechniken. Materialien und Geometrie kennzeichnen diese Platzhälfte als dem »modernen« Manchester zugehörig.

Die markante, skulpturale »Naht« für die beiden »Stoffe« bilden aneinander gereihte Rampen. Diesen Bruch in der Topographie des Ortes zu kitten, ist wohl der Knackpunkt des Entwurfs. Das vorgefundene, ziemlich komplizierte verschobene Niveau des Platzes bringt es mit sich, dass die Länge der Rampen variiert und jede ein bisschen höher liegt als die vorherige. Zusammen wirken die Rampen und Mauern wie riesige Rutschen und Leitern und bilden zugleich ein sanft ansteigendes Amphitheater. Die niedrigen, breiten Mauern, die jede Rampe begrenzen, bieten genügend Sitzfläche. Das Rampensystem ist vieldeutig: Es ist gleichermaßen der Hauptdurchgang für die Fußgänger wie auch der beste Ort zum Niederlassen und Ausspannen. So wird die »Naht« zum Ausdruck für Übergang und Wechsel und gleichzeitig zum belebtesten Bereich. Genau diese Spannung zwischen Alt und Neu, Auf und Ab, Bewegung und Innehalten macht den Platz spannend und gibt ihm sein eigenes Gesicht.

Vergebliche Liebesmüh. Der ursprüngliche Entwurf sah acht künstliche Palmen von zehn Meter Höhe vor, die in einer Reihe vor die Fassade des Kaufhauses gepflanzt werden sollten. Sie sollten aus Stahlmasten bestehen, gekrönt mit blauen Metallwedeln. Eben weil sie exotisch und nicht von dieser Welt zu sein schienen, sollten diese Palmen hier auf eine künftige Welt der unbegrenzten Möglichkeiten hindeuten und zugleich für Autos und Fußgänger auf ihrem Weg zum und vom Platz eine Schleuse bilden. Außerdem sollte die Anmutung der oberen, »neuen« Platzhälfte ins Sonderbare gesteigert werden. Die Gestaltungskommission jedoch, die über die künstlerischen Inhalte des Platzes entschied und sich nicht mit den Palmen anfreunden konnte, beschloss leider, sie wegzulassen. Wider unseren Rat ersetzten die Bauherren deshalb die Palmen durch Windrad-Skulpturen von anderen Designern.

per plaza. This reconciliation of the site's topography is the design's most powerful moment and fundamentally expresses an understanding of how Exchange Square is to be occupied. Because of the complex warping of the existing ground plane, each ramp varies in length and steps up slightly from the next. The collective ramps and walls create a giant "chutes and ladders" effect and form a gently curving amphitheatre. The low, wide walls that define each ramp provide ample seating areas. This great, low, ramp system is multivalent, functioning as the major place for pedestrian transition and movement, as well as providing the best place to sit and relax. The "seam," which expresses transition and change, is also the area of greatest activity. It is precisely the tension between the old and the new, the up and the down, the moving and the stationary, which generates interest and personality.

Love's labours lost. The original design included a line of eight 10-metre-high palm trees that was to extend along the facade of the department store. These palms were to be constructed from steel poles and topped with blue, laser-cut, metal fronds. They were to be used specifically for their exotic out-of-this-world image and to hint at a future world where anything goes. They were intended to spatially designate a gate through which cars and pedestrians would pass. They were to further the "new," and perhaps strange, nature of the upper plaza. Unfortunately, the palm trees were cut from the design by a design review committee that exerted control over the artistic content of the plaza. Against our judgement as the plaza designers, the committee chose to replace the blue palms with pinwheel structures designed by others.

Exchange Square, Manchester, Great Britain
Client: Manchester Millennium Ltd.
Master plan: EDAW
Design of the square: Martha Schwartz, Inc. (project team: Martha Schwartz, Shauna Gillies-Smith, Don Sharp, Paula Meijerink, Lital Fabian, Patricia Bales)
Size: 10,000 square metres
Completion: 1999
Costs: GBP 4 million

Lust auf Details

A fancy for details

In Switzerland it is common for architects, landscape architects, building clients, specialised engineers and other project participants to present each other with gifts at the end of the year as a token of gratitude.

When I began to set up a business in 1984 I was confronted with the issue of what I could send whom, how and why. Then I had the idea to use my own photographs. I have always had a passion for taking pictures on trips.

While photographing I put special emphasis on composition and choosing the frame for my subject. Over and again I discovered that one and the same subject taken from the same point by different people could result in very different photos – each with a very personal expression to it. Usually, however, people just go ahead and shoot – the main thing: the photos are in focus.

I am mainly interested in details and the materials that we encounter every day everywhere we go. They make up the character of a place. To recognise these details and to photograph them in an intriguing manner using light and shade, black-and-white or colour films, I feel, is an extremely sensuous job for art design. After that I enjoy sorting the prints, recognising the places according to the details, and to be happy about especially good pictures.

My motifs are graphical in nature and often are not immediately identifiable upon first glance. Only upon scrutiny does each person find his own interpretation.

I have been sending these photos for sixteen years, so in the year 2000 I have combined the sixteen subjects, one for every year, into a collage which has inspired the present gallery of pictures in Topos.

In der Schweiz ist es üblich, dass sich Architekten, Landschaftsarchitekten, Bauherren, Fachingenieure und andere Projektbeteiligte zum Jahreswechsel mit kleinen Aufmerksamkeiten untereinander für die gute Zusammenarbeit bedanken. Als ich mich 1984 selbständig machte, stand ich vor der Frage, was ich wem wie und warum schicken könnte. Ich kam auf die Idee, meine eigenen Fotos zu verwenden. Auf Reisen fotografierte ich stets leidenschaftlich gern. Besonders viel Wert legte ich auf den Bildaufbau und auf die Wahl des Bildausschnitts.

Immer wieder stellte ich fest, dass ein und dasselbe Sujet, von demselben Standpunkt von unterschiedlichen Personen aufgenommen, sehr unterschiedliche Fotos ergeben kann – jedes mit einem sehr persönlichen Ausdruck. Die meisten Hobby-Fotografen knipsen allerdings unsensibel drauflos, Hauptsache ihr Foto wird scharf. Das Ergebnis ist dann nichtssagend, spannungslos und ohne künstlerischen Ausdruck. Auf dem Bild sieht man Landschaften oder Städte wie aus der Ferne, oder aber die großen architektonischen Würfe eines Ortes. Alles Bilder, die in jedem beliebigen Bildband vorkommen könnten.

Mich interessieren die Details und die Materialien, die einem auf Schritt und Tritt im Alltag begegnen. Sie machen den Charakter eines Ortes aus. Diese Details zu erkennen, sie mit Licht und Schatten auf Schwarzweiß- oder Farbfilm spannungsvoll abzulichten, empfinde ich als äußerst sinnliche Gestaltungsaufgabe. Im Nachhinein genieße ich es, die Fotoabzüge zu sortieren, an bestimmten Details Orte wiederzuerkennen und mich über besonders gelungene Aufnahmen zu freuen. Diese jahrelange Arbeit am Bild schärft meine Sinne und beeinflusst auch Form, Gestalt und Materialien meiner Projekte in der Landschaftsarchitektur.

Was lag also näher, als Kunden und Kollegen Grußkarten mit Originalabzügen meiner Fotos zu senden? Ich wählte absichtlich Bildausschnitte, die keinen Bezug zu aktuellen Bauprojekten haben. Vielfach sind sie auf den ersten Blick nicht eindeutig zu identifizieren, sondern wirken als grafische Motive. Erst beim näheren Betrachten findet jeder seine eigene Interpretation. Sechzehn Jahre lang verschickte ich solche Fotos, im Jahr 2000 kombinierte ich die sechzehn Sujets der vorangegangenen Jahre zu einer Collage – von ihr ist die vorliegende Bildstrecke inspiriert.

Walter Vetsch
(photos and text)

Gestalterisches Arbeit mit Fotografien schärft die Sinne des Landschaftsarchitekten und beeinflusst Form und Materialien seiner Projekte.
Art work with photographs sharpens the senses of the landscape architect, and has an influence on the forms and materials he uses in his projects.

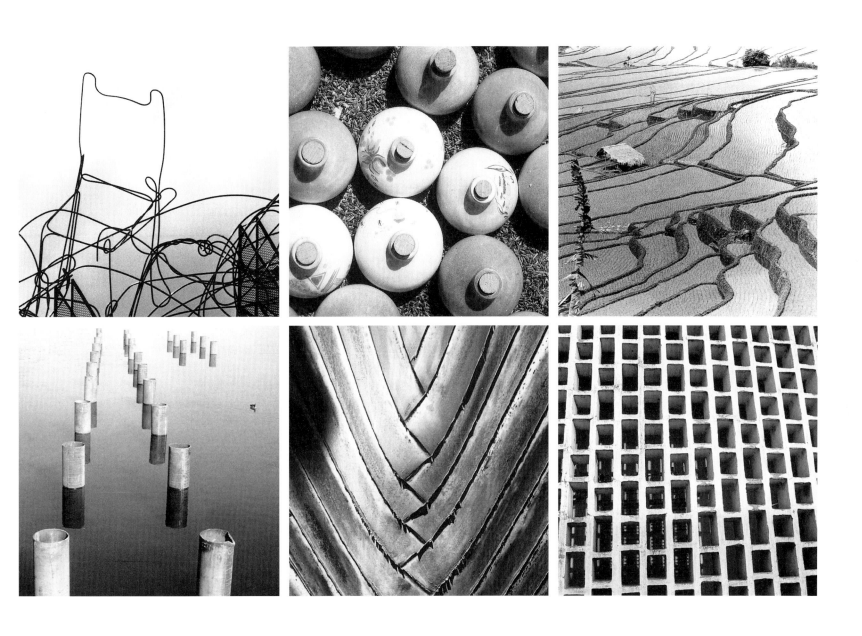

Schein und Wirklichkeit des Materials

Appearance and reality of the material

Bernard Lassus

Wer mit Materialien und ihren Erscheinungsformen spielt, kann kritische Landschaften erzeugen. Sie bieten der Öffentlichkeit, oder besser: den unterschiedlich denkenden Menschen einer örtlich begrenzten Gemeinschaft die Möglichkeit für Gedankenspiele, für Humor oder ironische Betrachtung der gewöhnlichen Wirklichkeit. Jedes Projekt ist ein Sonderfall, der in all seiner Komplexität studiert sein will und deshalb immer auch nach besonderen Antworten verlangt.

Kritische Landschaft: Die Brücke der Schlange und der Schmetterlinge. Zwei Landschaftsarchitekten der Stadt Istres im Großraum Marseille gaben mir den Auftrag, einen Entwurf für eine Fußgängerbrücke in einem städtischen Park zu erarbeiten. Die Stadt entwickelte gerade den Park, doch leider zerschnitt eine vierspurige Straße mit einem vier Meter breiten Mittelstreifen das Gelände – unnötig auszuführen, wie sehr der Park darunter litt, und ebenso unnötig, sich über die Gründe und Verantwortlichkeiten aufzuregen. Umso schlimmer, dass viele Kinder aus dem Viertel von der einen Seite des Parks zur Schule auf der anderen Seite gingen und dabei die Straße überqueren mussten. Es hatte bereits einige Unfälle gegeben, und die Stadt schickte seitdem zu Schulbeginn und -ende ein paar Polizisten in den Park, die den Kindern über die Straße halfen. Von Dauer konnte diese Lösung nicht sein – es galt also, eine Brücke zu bauen, um

Materialien sind mehr als ästhetisch wahrnehmbare Materie. Sie transportieren immer auch Bedeutungen, Wünsche, Urteile.

Materials are more than just perceptible matter. They always transport meanings, wishes and judgements as well.

Whoever plays with materials and their forms of appearances can produce critical landscapes. They offer the public – or more precisely, individuals of a locally defined community who think in different ways – opportunities for games of thought, humour or ironic perception of a common reality. Each project is a special case, which has to be studied in all of its complexity, and thus always calls for special answers.

Critical landscape: The bridge of the snake and the butterflies. Two landscape architects of the town of Istres in the region of Marseille offered me a contract to work out a design for a pedestrian bridge within an urban park. The town was developing the park, but, unfortunately, a four-lane road with a four metre wide central green strip cut through the area. It is unnecessary to enlarge on how badly the park was affected or even to get upset about the reasons and responsibilities involved. What makes things even worse is that many children from the neighbourhood on one side had to cross the street in order to get to their school on the other side of the park. There had been several accidents, and since then the town sent a few policemen to the park at the beginning and the end of school who helped the children cross the road. This could not work as a lasting solution, so the idea was to build a bridge in order to connect both sides of the park.

But which child would feel like ascending the bridge merely to descend on the other side? So in order that the children really use it the bridge could not just look like a bridge. A first proposal was rejected because the city thought it meant irony in the wrong place: The plan projected the construction of a wrought iron garden pavilion with a frieze of big butterflies with their antennae

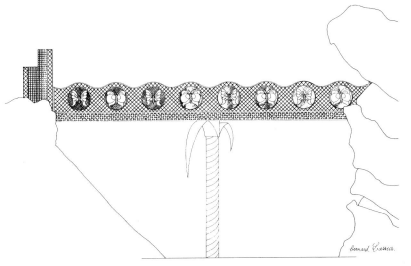

carrying lamps. The second proposal was put into construction: We designed a tunnel which looks as if hewn through a big rock, but actually it consists of a metal grid coated with concrete. Being about 40 metres long it extends across two lanes of the road as well as the central green strip. The other two lanes are spanned by a narrow, 15 metre long metal bridge. Its parapets carry interwoven metal ornaments with coloured butterfly motifs. My idea was not to make this artificial rock look any more real than the railway tunnel of my childhood painted over with cows on a meadow. The car drivers are probably wondering why they are driving through a rock while it would have been much easier to lead the road under the light metal bridge a few metres further to the side... The absurdity of the situation could have been easily concealed through a perfect metal bridge together with a few pine trees. But in this way it has been made obvious, for it would not have even crossed the drivers' minds that they were actually driving through a park. Must one not treat the absurd with something absurd in or-

die beiden Teile des Parks zu verbinden. Welches Kind aber hätte Lust, auf eine Brücke hinaufzusteigen, bloß um auf der anderen Seite wieder hinabzusteigen? Damit die Kinder sie wirklich benutzten, durfte die Brücke nicht so aussehen wie eine Brücke. Ein erster Vorschlag wurde verworfen, weil die Stadt ihn für Ironie am falschen Platz hielt: Der Plan sah den Bau eines schmiedeeisernen Gartenpavillons vor, mit einem Fries aus großen Schmetterlingen, deren Fühler Leuchten trugen. Der zweite Vorschlag wurde gebaut: Wir entwarfen einen Tunnel, der aussieht wie ein Felsen, in Wirklichkeit aber aus einem mit Beton verkleideten Metallgitter besteht. Etwa vierzig Meter lang, überdeckt er zwei Fahrspuren der Straße sowie den Mittelstreifen. Die zwei anderen Spuren überspannt eine schmale, fünfzehn Meter lange Metallbrücke. Ihre Brüstungen tragen farbige Schmetterlingsmotive aus Metallgeflecht. Meine Idee war, den falschen Felsen nicht »wirklicher« ausschauen zu lassen als den Eisenbahntunnel aus meiner Kinderzeit, den ein Gemälde mit Kühen auf einer Wiese zierte. Die Autofahrer wundern sich wahrscheinlich, warum sie durch einen Felsen hindurch fahren, wenn es doch viel einfacher gewesen wäre, die Straße ein paar Meter weiter seitlich unter der leichten Metallbrücke hindurchzuführen... So wird die Absurdität des Ortes deutlich, die eine formvollendete Brücke zusammen mit ein paar Pinien kaschiert hätte, denn die Autofahrer wären nicht einmal auf die Idee gekommen, dass sie einen Park queren.

Muss man dem Absurden nicht etwas noch Absurderes entgegensetzen, um Schein und Wirklichkeit zu enthüllen? Mein Problem bestand darin, den Kindern eine Brücke schmackhaft zu machen, dabei aber nicht zur Geisel einer Fehlentscheidung zu werden – das ist der Grund für diese Kritische Landschaft.

Pflanzen-Fassaden und Materialien für die Stadt Evry. Vor einigen Jahren bekam ich den Auftrag, die Fassaden einer Reihe Wohnhäuser zu entwerfen, die an einem Park in Evry bei Paris entstehen sollten. Ein Teil der Häuser sollte Sozialwohnungen beherbergen, der andere Eigentumswohnungen – für die Fassaden der letzteren waren Ziegel vorgesehen, für die der ersteren gestrichener Beton. Ich schlug vor, allen direkt am Park liegenden Fas-

Das Material gibt Auskunft über die Absicht des Gestalters: Ein künstlicher Felsen bestehend aus einem mit Beton verkleideten Metallgitter, verbindet die beiden Teile eines Parks in Istres – die Künstlichkeit des Felsens führt den Autofahrern augenzwinkernd die Absurdität der Situation vor.

The material reveals the intention of the designer: An artificial boulder consisting of a concrete coated metal grid links both parts of a park in Istres together – the artificiality of the boulder demonstrates the absurdity of the whole situation with a knowing wink of an eye.

der to reveal the connection between appearance and reality? My problem consisted in trying to make a bridge appeal to the children without at the same time being pinned down for having made a wrong decision. That is the rationale behind this critical landscape.

Plant facades and materials for the town of Evry. Several years ago I got an assignment to design the facades of a row of apartment houses which were to be developed along a park in Evry near Paris. Part of them were supposed to contain state-subsidised flats, while the others were to be divided up into condominiums. For the facades of the latter bricks were to be used. Those of the former were to consist of coated concrete. I suggested to give all of the facades facing the park a visual reference to the vegetation, and to use them in a sensitive way as material for the dwellers to perceive. The tenants were offered flower boxes with initial planting. Moreover, we designed a surface made of twisted cords, made a plastic mould for them, and applied it to the casing for the production of the concrete facade plates. The relief plates were finally given a light coat of green varnish. In order that the facade should also catch one's eye from the park we applied palm leaf motifs upon it – also in green. There was only 30 millimetres of room in depth for the reliefs in the casing, and the concrete was ready to be taken out of the casing twelve hours after pouring it. For the apartment house facades not facing the park, we made casts from real brick facades and created artificial ones out of concrete which was then painted in the colour shades of normal bricks. The artificial brick facades actually can not be distinguished from the neighbouring ones.

saden einen optischen Bezug zur Vegetation zu verleihen, und sie auf sensible Weise als Material zu verwenden, das die Bewohner wahrnehmen können. Den Mietern wurden Blumenkästen mit einer Erstbepflanzung angeboten. Zudem gestalteten wir eine Oberfläche aus gedrehten Kordeln, fertigten einen Kunststoffabguss und brachten ihn auf der Schalung an, die zur Herstellung der Beton-Fassadenplatten diente. Die Reliefplatten erhielten anschließend eine leichte grüne Lasur. Damit die Fassade auch vom Park aus ins Auge fällt, setzten wir Palmwedel-Motive auf, ebenfalls in Grün. Für die Reliefs gab es in der Schalung nur einen Spielraum von 30 Millimetern, und der Beton wurde bereits zwölf Stunden nach dem Einbringen ausgeschalt. Für die Mietshaus-Fassaden, die nicht zum Park zeigen, machten wir Abgüsse von echten Ziegelfassaden und schufen falsche aus Beton, der in den Farbtönen von Backstein gestrichen wurde. Die falschen Ziegelfassaden lassen sich von ihren Nachbarn nicht unterscheiden.

Bei der Fassadengestaltung von parknahen Wohnhäusern in Evry galt es, die Nähe zur Natur zu unterstreichen. Dabei diente ein Kunststoffabguss aus gedrehten Kordeln als Vorlage für die Beton-Fassadenplatten, die grün gestrichen und mit einem Palmwedel verziert wurden.

Concerning the facade design of apartment houses near a park in Evry the idea was to emphasise their closeness to nature. In doing so a plastic casting of curly cords served as a mould for the concrete facade plates which were painted green and adorned with a palm leaf motif.

Produktentwicklung mit Aluminium

Production development with aluminium

Why do landscape architects occupy themselves with developing products – and then, on top of that, out of aluminium? All gardens, parks, places and recreational areas are designed products. Within these there are further landscaping elements such as trees, shrubs, pavements, steel, wood or glass constructions and the whole range of the so-called landscaping equipment. Whoever has worked with the products of various companies for several years, tends to discard them bit by bit since most of them do not suit individual requests according to form, function or variability, or they are simply outmoded. And, finally, one starts to make things with one's own hands – at first in a conventional craftsman-like way, which is expensive and yet not exactly a great success. Such home-made developments can be refined on any construction site, but the required design and functional perfection is not forthcoming.

There comes the time when both one's anger and curiosity rises to the point where one does not want anything more than the development of a matured and ready-made industrial product that provides a wide range of applications, for example, modular construction systems which are individually adaptable, extendable, variable and good-looking. They should be better than what the market has to offer, moreover, innovative and future-oriented.

Landscape architects are often sceptical about uncustomary building materials, especially aluminium on account of its prima facie high primary energy costs. Since there is no such thing as inherently bad material, but rather wrong applications and bad designs, we were intrigued by the idea to work with this material.

Bernd Krüger

Weshalb beschäftigen sich Landschaftsarchitekten mit der Entwicklung von Produkten, und dann auch noch aus Aluminium? Alle Gärten, Parks, Plätze und Freizeitanlagen sind gestaltete Produkte. In ihnen gibt es weitere Gestaltungselemente, wie Bäume, Sträucher, Bodenbeläge, Stahl-, Holz- und Glaskonstruktionen, und die breite Palette der sogenannten Ausstattung. Wer einige Jahre mit den Erzeugnissen verschiedener Hersteller gearbeitet hat, sortiert immer mehr aus, da die meisten Produkte nicht den individuellen Wünschen nach Form, Funktion und Variabilität entsprechen oder veraltet sind. Und schließlich fängt man selber an zu basteln - zuerst auf biedere handwerkliche Art, was teuer ist und trotzdem nicht das Gelbe vom Ei liefert. Solche Eigenentwicklungen lassen sich dann auf

Wenn der Markt nicht die passenden Ausstattungselemente für den Freiraum bietet, sind Ideen für eigene Entwicklungen gefragt.

Whenever the market does not offer the suiting landscaping elements for open space, ideas to make one's own developments are called for.

Ein Bild und ein Bambustrog begrenzen den Essplatz im Hausgarten Schuldt in Sindelfingen. Ihre Rahmen bestehen aus Aluminium-Scharnierpfosten mit Aufstecknasen. Eingehängt sind geometrisch gestaltete Plexiglasscheiben beim Bild, Metallbleche beim Pflanzgefäß.

A picture and a bamboo trough frame the eating place of a family's house garden in Sindelfingen. Their frames consist of aluminium hinge posts with fastening joints. Attached to these are geometrically designed acrylic glass panes for the picture and metal foils for the plant container.

jeder Baustelle zwar verfeinern, aber die gewünschte gestalterische und funktionale Perfektion kommt nicht dabei heraus. Irgendwann werden Ärger und Neugier so groß, dass man sich nichts lieber wünscht als die Entwicklung serienreifer Industrieprodukte, die eine große Bandbreite von Anwendungen bieten – Baukastensysteme also, individuell und erweiterbar, variabel, einfach, kostengünstig und schön. Sie sollen besser sein als das, was der Markt hergibt, innovativ und zukunftsträchtig. Die Produkte sollen dauerhaft, ökologisch sinnvoll und kombinierbar mit anderen Bauelementen sein.

Landschaftsarchitekten stehen ungewohnten Baumaterialien oft skeptisch gegenüber, dem Aluminium allemal wegen seines oberflächlich betrachtet hohen Aufwandes an Primärenergie. Da es kein an sich schlechtes Material gibt, sondern bloß falsche Anwendungen und Gestaltungen, reizte uns die Auseinandersetzung mit diesem Werkstoff.

What is aluminium? This light metal is the third most common element of the earth's crust after oxygen and silicon. It is extracted from bauxite by means of sodium hydroxide, and processed into aluminium oxide. Primary aluminium then emerges through fused mass electrolysis. The primary energy costs for one ton of aluminium is about six times as high as that for a ton of steel. But since the material's density of 2.7 is particularly slight, only twice the amount in energy costs are to be expected. Moreover, in contrast to steel, more than half of the world's aluminium production is based on regenerative water power. The waste products accumulated dur-

Die Idee für das Handlauf-System stammt aus dem Mastbau für Segelboote. Der Pfosten besteht aus einem Aluminium-Strangpressprofil mit Einschubnuten für T-Elemente, auf denen Spanndrähte befestigt sind. Bei den Rankmasten stecken die Abstandshalter in der Schiebenut. Die Treppenwange besteht wie die Müllplatzeinfassung (gegenüber) aus Borderprofilen.

The idea of a hand rail system comes from the construction of masts for sailboats. The posts consist of an aluminium continuous casting profile with slide-on grooves for T-elements upon which suspended cables are attached. The spacing elements are inserted into the groove. The side of the step case consists of border profiles like those of the waste disposal casing (opposite).

ing production are recycled, or are reprocessed for industrial use. More than 30 percent of the aluminium produced world-wide is recycled material that only requires five percent of the energy needed for crude aluminium. If one realises that the material has an extremely long life span and is easy to transport and install due to its light weight, quite a lot can be said in favour of aluminium on the basis of its overall energy balance.

This working material can be easily processed as well: One can knead and forge it, make parts through sand, gravity, and pressure die casting or by means of continuous casting profiles. By adding small amounts of other metals like magnesium, manganese, copper, chromium or titanium alloys are produced with different kinds of properties ranging from brittle to highly elastic when produced with narrow cross sections. The surfaces can be worked on mechanically, and can be pressed, stamped, cut, polished, coated, anodised or refined in other ways.

Production development. The first step is always the most difficult. One has a vision and many ideas. The industry smiles at the gardener, and the sales company speaks of lacking acceptance on the market and the gigantic PR-investments required. In the beginning both try to get rid of the intruder in order to secure their own advantage. After that the patent lawyers, business consultants, contract experts and other fee chargers come. Then come the investments in time, ideas, sketches, tool drawings, PR-considerations, models, test series, certificates, prototype developments and so forth until the first product emerges. Trust in God is called for since nobody gives any money, everybody is waiting for cash flow without risk, and one hopes that the next

Was ist Aluminium? Nach Sauerstoff und Silizium ist das Leichtmetall das dritthäufigste Element der Erdkruste. Es wird mit Natronlauge aus Bauxit herausgelöst und zu Aluminiumoxid (Tonerde) verarbeitet. Mittels Schmelzflusselektrolyse entsteht anschließend Primäraluminium. Der primäre Energieaufwand für eine Tonne Aluminium ist etwa sechsmal so hoch wie für eine Tonne Stahl – da das Material mit einem spezifischen Gewicht von 2,7 aber ausgesprochen leicht ist, muss man nur mit dem doppelten Energieaufwand rechnen. Im Gegensatz zu Stahl wird zudem heute über die Hälfte der Welt-Aluminiumproduktion mit regenerativer Wasserkraft hergestellt. Die Abfallstoffe der Produktion werden recycelt oder in der Industrie weiterverwendet. Über dreißig Prozent des weltweit produzierten Aluminiums ist recyceltes Material, das nur noch fünf Prozent der Energie von Rohaluminium bedarf. Denkt man daran, dass das Material eine extrem lange Lebensdauer hat, unendlich oft zu recyceln ist, keine

Aluminium products in the Schuldt Garden, Sindelfingen, Germany
Client: Bea and Rainer Schuldt, Sindelfingen
Design: Bernd Krüger from Krüger + Möhrle landscape architects, Stuttgart
Construction: 1999 – 2000

Schadstoffe an die Umwelt abgibt und durch sein geringes Gewicht günstig zu transportieren und einzubauen ist, so spricht in der Gesamtenergiebilanz vieles für Aluminium. Auch verarbeiten lasst sich der Werkstoff ideal: Man kann ihn kneten und schmieden, Sand-, Kokillen- und Druckgussteile oder Strangpressprofile herstellen. Durch den Zusatz geringer Mengen anderer Metalle wie Magnesium, Mangan, Kupfer, Chrom oder Titan entstehen Legierungen mit verschiedenen Eigenschaften von extrem spröde bis hochelastisch bei geringen Querschnitten. Die Oberflächen können mechanisch bearbeitet, gestanzt, geprägt, geschliffen, poliert, beschichtet, eloxiert oder sonstwie veredelt werden.

Produktentwicklung. Aller Anfang ist schwer. Man hat eine Vision und viele Ideen. Die Industrie belächelt den »Gärtner«, und die Vertriebsfirma spricht von mangelnder Marktakzeptanz und gigantischen PR-Vorleistungen. Beide versuchen erst einmal, den »Eindringling« abzuwimmeln, um den eigenen Vorteil zu sichern. Dann kommen die Behörden, Patentanwälte, Wirtschaftsberater, Vertragsspezialisten und die sonstigen Gebührensammler. Dann die Vorleistungen an Zeit, Ideen, Skizzen, Werkzeugzeichnungen, PR-Überlegungen, Modellen, Versuchsserien, Prüfzeugnissen, Prototypentwicklungen und so weiter und so fort, bis das erste Erzeugnis marktreif ist. Gottvertrauen ist angesagt, denn keiner gibt Geld, alle warten auf Cash-Flow ohne Risiko und man selber hofft, dass die kommenden zwei oder drei Jahre die Investitionen wieder hereinbringen und genügend Spielraum lassen für weitere Produktfamilien, die im Gehirn oder auf dem Skizzenblock warten. Denn trotz allem lässt einen diese Arbeit nicht mehr los.

Das Liner-System. Seit Jahren haben wir uns über die gängigen Abgrenzungen geärgert, welche Wege oder Plätze zu ihrer Umgebung hin abschotten. Borde mit Streifenfundamenten lassen sich nur schwer entfernen, der Rasen am Rande wird braun, und die Feuchtigkeit ist abgesperrt. Die herkömmlichen Stahl- oder Alubänder mit angeschweißten Laschen und Punktfundamenten waren uns nicht steif oder elastisch genug, zu kompliziert sowie unflexibel im Einbau. Unser neues System lässt sich ohne Fundamente in den Unterbau nageln und auf Dächern verlegen, vor Ort korrigieren, ineinanderstecken, auf Klemmplatten klipsen und bildet optisch kaum eine Barriere. Der Industriedesigner Viktor Bremzay perfektionierte

two or three years will bring in the desired returns and leave enough time for further types of products in one's mind or on paper waiting to be realised. For, despite everything this kind of work does not let you go.

The liner system. For years we have been irritated by the current fringes that separate paths or squares from their surroundings. Borders with strip foundations are difficult to remove. The lawn at the edge becomes brown, and the moisture is cut off. The current steel or aluminium bands with welded loops and point foundations have not been stiff or elastic enough, and have been too complicated and inflexible to install. Our new system can be nailed into the lower layer without foundations, it can be corrected, interconnected, attached to clamp plates, and it forms a visual barrier. The industrial designer Viktor Bremzay perfected the system. We had it patented, and are meanwhile developing increasingly more parts for installation as well as connecting elements.

The border system. Over and over again we had problems with the troughs and bed borders on light weight roofs that were supposed to look attractive and suit the current architectural taste. Our system for which we are currently applying for a patent is based on a hinge post device. This involves connecting the base plates through pipes in order to suit static requirements and to prevent damage to the roof sheeting. The hinge posts can be positioned according to any angle, and can be extended upwards as fixtures of any kind. There are two distinct view surfaces, and, instead of the two centimetre thick cavity-structured walls, plates made of glass, wood or granite can be installed. Everything is wonderfully light. In the

Um Parkplätze besser auszunutzen, können die einzelnen Stellflächen mit Anfahrschwellen markiert werden. Ein dreieckiger Alu-Hohlkörper lässt sich dafür auf eine Grundplatte aus Aluminium klipsen. In die sichtbaren Anfahrflächen können Profilbleche eingeschoben werden, geprägt oder bedruckt mit Autonummern, Werbung...

Each of the parking spaces can be marked with drive thresholds in order to save space. A triangular aluminium hollow case can be clipped onto an aluminium ground plate. In the visible drive areas profiled foils stamped or painted with company names, licence plate numbers or advertisements can be slid on.

meantime we are building many variations ranging from carport roofs, waste disposal areas, sand box frames, steps to picture frames.

Drive thresholds, car-stop. Whoever has seen or planned parking places has invariably encountered the same problem: The car spaces are not used properly, and are not adequately marked. Neither screwed-in oak beams nor ready-made concrete slabs nailed into the foundations producing drive inclines meet the mark. Here we had the idea to use a base plate of aluminium which can also be installed later. One can then clamp in a triangular aluminium hollow body against which the cars gently roll onto. In the visible areas of the drive one can install structured and profiled metal sheets which may be stamped or engraved with company logos, for guest parking or with advertisements. Each parking space is enclosed by stamped strips of sheeted metal on the sides railed into grooves. We developed this product with industrial designers, too.

Railing and banister systems. The idea was taken from the constructions of the masts of sail boats although we are no yachtspeople. The posts consist of anodised, rounded profiles made by continuous casting with four grooves designed for insertion arranged in a cross-wise fashion. They can be fastened onto the wall with screw plates, or they can be embedded into a concrete cast. T-shaped profiles to which elements of wood, glass, lath wood, metal, fabric or cables can be attached can in turn be railed into the grooves.

The fixtures for railings are also based on this system. Of course, one can use the railing or the posts by themselves, and combine them with other profiles of steel, wood or plastic.

das System. Wir ließen es patentieren und entwickeln inzwischen immer mehr Aufsteckteile und Verbindungselemente.

Das Border-System. Immer wieder hatten wir Probleme mit Trögen und Beetabgrenzungen auf Dächern, die ein geringes Gewicht besitzen, gut aussehen und zur zeitgenössischen Architektur passen sollten. Unser zum Patent angemeldetes System beruht auf einer Scharnierpfosten-Konstruktion, die in Rohre auf Bodenplatten gesteckt wird, damit die Statik stimmt und die Dachhaut nicht beschädigt wird. Die Scharnierpfosten ermöglichen jeden Winkel und können als Halterungen aller Art nach oben verlängert werden. Es gibt zwei verschiedene Sichtflächen, statt der zwei Zentimeter starken Hohlkammerwände lassen sich auch Platten aus Glas, Holz oder Granit einsetzen. Alles ist wunderbar leicht. Inzwischen bauen wir viele Varianten – seien es Regalböden, Carport-Dächer, Müllplätze, Lampenaufhängungen, Sandkasteneinfassungen, Treppenstufen oder Bilderrahmen.

Anfahrschwelle »Auto-Stop«. Wer viele Parkplätze gesehen und geplant hat, trifft immer wieder auf das gleiche Problem: Die Stellplätze werden nicht ausgenutzt und sind unzureichend markiert. Weder eingeschraubte Eichenbalken noch in den Unterbau genagelte Beton-Fertigteile mit Anfahrschräge sind der Hit. Da kam uns die Idee einer multifunktionalen Grundplatte aus Aluminium, die auch nachträglich eingebaut und mit Bodennägeln fixiert werden kann. Auf diese Platte lässt sich ein dreieckiger Alu-Hohlkörper klipsen, gegen den die Autos sanft anrollen. In die sichtbaren Anfahrflächen können strukturierte Profilbleche eingeschoben werden, geprägt oder bedruckt, mit dem Firmenkennzeichen, als Gästeparkplatz oder mit Werbung. Seitlich schließt ein gestanztes, in Nuten eingeschobenes Blech den Hohlkörper ab. Auch dieses Produkt entwickelten wir gemeinsam mit dem Industriedesigner.

Reling-System. Die Idee für dieses Handlauf- und Geländersystem stammt aus dem Mastbau für Segelboote. Der Pfosten besteht aus einem eloxierten, rundlichen Strangpressprofil mit vier kreuzweise angeordneten Einschubnuten. Er kann mit Schraubplatten an der Wand befestigt oder einbetoniert werden. In die Nuten lassen sich T-förmige Profile schieben, in die wiederum Elemente aus Holz, Glas, Latten, Metall, Textil oder Spanndrähte eingehängt werden. Auch die Halterung des Handlaufs entwickelt sich aus T-Profil. Selbstverständlich kann man auch nur den Handlauf oder nur den Pfosten verwenden und sie mit anderen Profilen aus Stahl, Holz oder Kunststoff ergänzen.

Magisches Wasser in Ostwestfalen

Magical water in Westphalia

Henri Bava

Zur Landesgartenschau in Bad Oeynhausen und Löhne holten die Planer von Agence Ter das unterirdische Heilwasser der Kurregion ans Licht. For the regional garden show in Bad Oeynhausen und Löhne, the Agence Ter planners brought subterranean water out into the open.

Statt üppige Blumenbilder nach dem Geschmack der meisten Besucher einer Landesgartenschau zu komponieren, haben wir uns entschieden, wie bei all unseren Projekten vor allem

das Charakteristische des Grundstücks herauszuarbeiten, um dem Ort auf der Gemeindegrenze von Bad Oeynhausen und Löhne Identität zu verleihen. Was diesen Ort ausmacht, ist nicht sofort sichtbar, denn es befindet sich unter der Erdoberfläche: das Wasser. Wir nannten es »magisch«, da es heilend wirkt. Auf diesem Wasser gründet die Wirtschaft der Region, seinetwegen sind hier Thermen und Kliniken entstanden. Gleichzeitig verbannen Thermen und Kliniken das Wasser aber auch in die Welt der Heilanstalten. Uns lag deshalb daran, das Wasser aus dem klammen Halbdunkel dieser Anstalten ans Licht und unter den freien Himmel zu holen.

Selbst wenn das Wasser in der Erde verborgen bleibt, ist es nicht weniger wirklich. Hydrogeologen haben seine Ströme kartiert – entlang unterirdischer Verwerfungslinien, die erstaunlich parallel verlaufen. Das Wasser an sich ist nichts weiter als eine Abstraktion des Materials, in dem es fließt, sich entwickelt und von dem es sich lenken lässt: der Erde. Wenn wir also für das vergängliche Schauspiel einer Gartenschau das omnipräsente, aber kaum sichtbare Wasser in Szene setzen, dann nur im Zusammenspiel mit seinem Grund, der Erde, die schließlich unser aller Grund ist. Wir arbeiteten deshalb in der dritten Dimension, in der Tiefe der Boden-

Instead of luxuriant beds of flowers that appeal to the taste of most regional garden show visitors, we decided - as in all our projects - to concentrate on the characteristic element of the site and thus underscore its identity. Water, the element of the site in question, located between the towns of Bad Oeynhausen and Löhne in Westphalia, northern Germany, was not immediately apparent, since it exists below the surface of the

earth. We called it "magical" as it is healing in effect. It forms the basis of the regional economy, and has led to the establishment of thermal baths and clinics. At the same time, thermal baths and clinics keep the water concealed within their walls, and it thus became our intention to bring the water out into the open. Hydrogeologists have mapped its flow along subterranean faults that run in astonishingly parallel lines. As such, the water is nothing other than an abstract version of the earth, the material in which it flows, builds up and allows itself to be guided. In other words, if we wanted to stage the omnipresent but scarcely visible element of water as the focus of the very temporary spectacle of a garden show, we had to do this in interaction with the earth, the basis and foundation not only of water but of all life on this planet. For this reason, we worked in the third dimension, plunging down into the depths of the earth's strata and reaching upwards towards the sky. For this reason, all the resulting water gardens are dug into the earth. This excavation work involved scratching the surface in some places, and gouging out great holes in others, as for the Water Crater, and came to stand for the search for the 'truth' of the site. At other places we piled earth onto earth, thus creating 'artificial' places to underscore the artificiality of the event. The World Climate Avenue, the main axis of the garden show park, therefore rises out of the

fields like an elongated platform, viewing terrace and stage all in one, and features embankment walls faced in Cor-Ten steel to emphasise the man-made character of the avenue. Flower gardens, nursery gardens, cemetery gardens and other classical garden show elements are located on level ground, between the two extremes of the downward-looking and upward-striving landscape interventions. This gives the various gardens on the fertile earth a 'normal' touch, an ele-

schichten und in der Höhe der Aufbauten. So sind die Wassergärten allesamt in die Erde eingegraben – dazu mussten wir Boden abtragen, manchmal nur oberflächlich, manchmal metertief, wie beim Wasserkrater. Das Graben und Ausschneiden steht für die Suche nach der »Wahrheit« des Ortes. An anderer Stelle hingegen fügten wir Erde hinzu, schütteten Boden auf und setzten der Landschaft »künstliche« Orte auf, um die Künstlichkeit der Gartenschau zu betonen. Die Hauptachse des Gartenschauparks, die Allee des Weltklimas, hebt sich deshalb als langgestreckter Podest aus den Feldern heraus, Aussichtsterrasse und riesige Bühne für die Gärten zugleich. Ihre Stützmauern aus Corten-Stahl unterstreichen das Menschengemachte der Anlage. Zwischen den beiden Extremen, der nach innen gekehrten und der ausgestellten Landschaft, befinden sich auf ebener Erde Blumengärten, Baumschulgärten, Friedhofsgärten – die klassische Palette der Gartenschau. Ihr kommt der Status des »Normalen« zu, schlicht auf dem fruchtbaren Grund angelegt, wie die Äcker nebenan.

Das sprudelnde, lebendige, launenhafte und beinahe gefährliche Wasser lässt sich besonders im Hohlraum des Wasserkraters erleben. Das Spektakel eröffnet sich einem nicht auf den ersten Blick. Da das Wasser in der Erde verborgen ist, muss man an einen Ort hinabsteigen, der beim Betreten im Ungewissen liegt. Ankommende sehen zunächst nur eine wogende Fläche, nämlich die Baumkronen einer Gruppe Felsenbirnen, die in einem Senkgarten rund um den Krater ge-

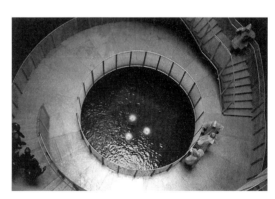

pflanzt sind. Die Baumkronen verlängern die Ebene der Wiese, über die man sich nähert. Eine Rampe und eine Treppe führen fünf Meter hinab in den Senkgarten, man gleitet unter die Bäume

Auf der Suche nach dem Wasser steigen die Besucher im Krater 18 Meter tief unter die Erdoberfläche. Wände aus Gabionen und Treppen aus galvanisiertem Stahl vermitteln das Rohe des Untergrundes. Aus dem Bassin schießt eine Fontäne durch die Öffnung des Eingangsplateaus, zur Einweihung bewundert von Bauherr, Politikern und zwei der Planer (standesgemäß in Schwarz).

In search of the water, visitors descend 18 metres below ground level inside the crater. Walls covered with gabions and stairs of galvanised steel express underground roughness. A fountain shoots up from the pool through the opening in the entrance platform. Onlookers at the inauguration include the client, politicians and two of the planners (up to standard in black).

Wasserbohrloch · Bewasserungsgarten · Wasserpflanzengarten · Spruhgarten · Weserklinie · Beginn der Allee des Wärtklimas · Querschnitt der Themengärten

Schnitt durch das Garten-
schaugelände mit Bodenauf-
bauten und Vertiefungen
(ganz oben), Schnitt durch den
Wasserkrater.

Cross-section of the garden
exhibition grounds shows the
raised and sunken elements
(top above); cross-section of
the Water Crater.

und läuft auf das Zentrum des Gartens zu. Riesige Corten-Stahl-Mauern umschließen es – sie sind nur der obere Rand eines in die Erde versenkten Kegels, die Wände eines enormen Brunnen-Bohrlochs. Auf der Innenseite sind diese Wände mit Gabionen verkleidet, über die das Wasser bis zum 18 Meter tief gelegenen Grund hinabrieselt.

Formen und Materialien im Inneren sind bewusst roh gehalten, wie auf der Baustelle. Einfache, schmucklose Treppen aus galvanisiertem Stahl winden sich spiralförmig in die Tiefe. Ein wenig unheimlich ist einem beim Abstieg zumute – zwischen den rohen Mauern, in der Nähe des gurgelnden Wassers, beim Zurückblicken nach oben zu dem kreisrunden Ausschnitt, der das Tageslicht in die Tiefe schickt wie ein Spot einen Lichtstrahl. In der Geschichte der Gartenkunst hat es solche Orte schon früh gegeben – der Oeynhauser Wasserkrater lässt sich auch als zeitgenössische Variante des römischen Nymphäums lesen. Man kann sich versenken in diesen geschlossenen Raum, einen Hortus conclusus, um mit dem ganzen Körper und mit allen Sinnen jenes erstaunliche Element Wasser zu erleben.

ment of simplicity like the neighbouring fields. At the garden show, the lively, moody and almost threatening character of water can be experienced most closely within the deep cavity of the Water Crater. The spectacle involved does not reveal itself at a first glance. Since the water is hidden in the earth, visitors have to descend down into unknown places. At first all they see is the swaying canopy made up of the tops of amelanchiers planted into a sunken garden around the inside the crater, their tops acting as a continuation of the fields across which the crater is approached. A ramp and a stairway lead five metres down into the sunken garden. From here visitors continue along beneath the trees to the centre of the garden. This features the tops of gigantic walls made of Cor-Ten steel that line a tapered hole, an enormous well, that plunges 18 metres into the earth. The insides of the walls are faced with gabions, down which the water trickles.

The materials deep down inside this crater have been left in a deliberately rough hewn shape, as if at a construction site. Simple and unadorned stairs made of galvanised steel spiral their way to the bottom of the drill-hole. Making the descent between the rough-hewn walls and close to the gurgling water is a little eerie, and a look up to the surface reveals a circle of sky, with the light shining down like the beams of a spotlight. Such places have long existed in the history of garden design, and thus the Oeynhausen Water Crater can be regarded as a modern version if the Roman nymphaeum.

One can immerse oneself in this closed space, this *hortus conclusus,* to experience that astonishing and vital element of water with the whole of one's body and all of one's senses.

Water Crater at the regional garden show 2000 in Bad Oeynhausen and Löhne, Germany
Client: Landesgartenschaugesellschaft Bad Oeynhausen und Löhne
Landscape architects: Agence Ter, Paris (Henri Bava, Olivier Philippe, Michel Hoessler)
with Alexander Bölk (project head)
Competition: 1998
Planning: 1998 – 2000
Construction: 1999 – 2000
Costs: DEM 5 million (Water Crater), DEM 55 million (park in total)

Hannover: Gärten der Materialvielfalt

Hannover: Gardens of material diversity

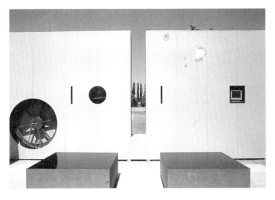  

World's fairs are like other architecture and garden festivals in that they provide opportunities for experimentation and space for creativity for architects and landscape architects. But there is also the danger of cluttering up a design concept beyond recognition with too many materials and products.

In his gardens for the Expo in Hannover, the Berlin landscape architect Kamel Louafi has managed to combine a large number of unusual materials into a clear picture. Moreover, the new open spaces are to outlast the Expo and they meet the demand for future prospects as neither the event nor the buildings do in their present form. For while the pavilions are going to be dismantled, the Gardens of Change, the Expo Park South and the Parc Agricole will only really develop with time.

The Gardens of Change form a green corridor 45 metres wide and 754 metres long extending between the pavilions. Here visitors can plunge into a world of garden motifs. As early as in his competition entry, Kamel Louafi insisted on the concept of change: from dark to light, from crowded to spacious, from artificial to natural.

Weltausstellungen bieten ebenso wie andere Bau- und Garten-Festivals die Chance zum Experiment und Raum für Kreativität – aber auch das Risiko, ein gestalterisches Konzept mit Materialien und Produkten bis zur Unkenntlichkeit zu überfrachten. Dem Berliner Landschaftsarchitekten Kamel Louafi ist es in seinen Gärten für die Hannoveraner Expo gelungen, eine Vielzahl ungewöhnlicher Materialien zu einem klaren Bild zu fügen. Die neuen Freiräume werden die Expo überdauern und dem Ruf nach Zukunft gerecht, den weder das Event noch die Architektur in dieser Form erfüllen. Denn während die Pavillons wieder abgebaut werden, können sich die »Gärten im Wandel«, der »Expo-Park-Süd« und der »Parc Agricole« mit der Zeit entfalten. Das Band der »Gärten im Wandel« verläuft als 45 Meter breiter und gut 750 Meter langer Grünfinger zwischen den Pavillons. Hier tauchen die Besucher ein in eine Welt der Gartenmotive. Schon im Wettbewerbsentwurf formulierte Kamel Louafi sein starkes Konzept: von dunkel nach hell, von dicht nach weit, von künstlich nach natürlich. Mit ausgewählten Materialien brachte er dieses Konzept vom Papier ins Gelände. Auf grauen dänischen Betonplatten schreiten wir einer Piazza zu, flankiert von dicht gepflanzten Schwarzkiefern, unter denen dunkelgrauer Diabas-Schotter liegt, in den wiederum Felsen aus grauem Gneis eingebettet sind. Etwa ein Viertel der Betonplatten ließ Louafi riffeln. Dadurch wirkt die Fläche in Schrägaufsicht dunkler. Auf der Piazza werden die Besucher von einer etwa zwei Meter hohen, strahlend blauen Betonwand

Stefan Leppert

Von dunkel nach hell, von dicht nach weit: In den Expo-Gärten von Kamel Louafi gibt es einige ungewöhnliche Materialien zu bewundern. From dark to light, from crowded to spacious: some unusual materials can be admired in the Expo gardens by Kamel Louafi.

Stein, Putz und Sand kennzeichnen die »Schleusen«, eine Reihe Garten-Folies, die in den »Gärten im Wandel« thematische Akzente setzen: das Maschinenhaus mit schwarzen Granitskulpturen (oben links), der Patio mit einem zentralen Bassin und dem Schattenwurf der Pergola-Holzkassetten (oben Mitte), das Sandhaus im Dünengarten.

Stone, stucco and sand distinguish the so-called "sluice gates," a series of follies accenting different themes in the Gardens of Change: the Machine House with black granite sculptures (top left), the Patio with a central pool and the shadows of the pergola's wooden panels (top centre), the Sand House in the Dune Garden.

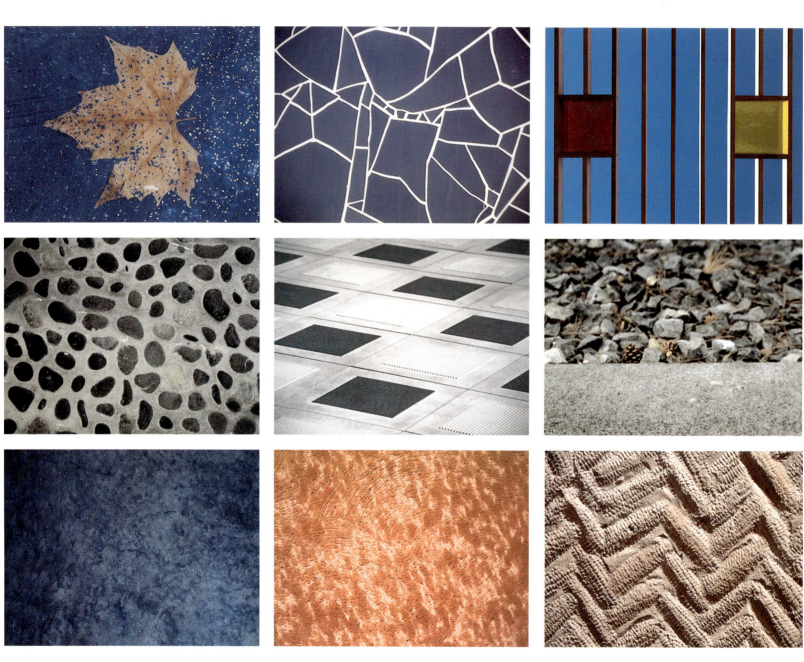

Auf der Expo-Piazza reizt eine blaue Betonwand zum Betasten (gegenüber oben). Das Auge gleitet über den Belag aus dänischen Betonplatten, von denen einige durch Riffelung dunkler erscheinen (oben Mitte). Von der Piazza steigt man zu den »Gärten im Wandel« hinab – durch einen Wasserfall (gegenüber), der wie ein Vorhang vor einer Wand aus blauen Megaceranfliesen hängt und mit den seitlichen, ockerfarbenen Putzflächen kontrastiert (gegenüber unten). Dieser Farbkontrast wiederholt sich: Weg durch den Klanggarten (gegenüber unten) mit eingeschlossenen Blättern (oben), Megaceran-Mosaik, Patio-Pergola, Belag aus isländischen Flusskieseln, Basaltschotter, geölter Tadelakkalkputz, Tierrafina-Lehmputz, afrikanischer Reliefputz.

A blue concrete wall on the Piazza at the Expo is tempting to touch (opposite top). Your eye sweeps across the paving of Danish concrete tiles, some of which appear darker because their surface was fluted (top centre). From the Piazza you descend to the Gardens of Change through a waterfall (opposite) suspended like a curtain in front of a wall of blue "Megaceran" tiles and contrasting with the ochre-coloured stucco surfaces on either side (opposite below). Such colour contrasts are repeated: path through the Garden of Sounds (opposite below) with enclosed leaves (top), "Megaceran" mosaic, Patio pergola, paving of Icelandic riverbed gravel, crushed basalt, oiled "tadelak" stucco, "tierrafina" mud stucco, African relief stucco.

Selected materials transferred the concept from the drawing board to the grounds.

On our way to the Piazza we walk along on Danish grey concrete tiles flanked by closely planted black pines. The ground under the trees is covered with dark grey crushed diabase, with grey gneiss rocks embedded in it. Louafi had about one quarter of the concrete tiles fluted. This makes the surface look darker when seen from an angle.

On the Piazza the visitor is drawn to an approximately two-metre-high, bright blue, concrete wall. Most people are tempted to touch it. Such experiences with textures recur in the so-called "sluice gates," which are the follies in the garden. On the one hand there is rough, earth-coloured "tierrafina" stucco and on the other "tadelak" stucco, smooth as glass and painted blue. The latter, a traditional kind of oiled lime stucco, is still common in Morocco and Andalusia today.

At the southern end of the Piazza paved with English sandstone setts, we look down from the Belvedere onto the Gardens of Change. A waterfall below us, three metres high and as wide as the whole garden, runs over the edge of a high-grade steel basin and falls into a pool, swallowing up the noise of the Expo. Its curtain of water hangs in front of huge, sapphire blue, ceramic tiles made of "Megaceran." These tiles, only seven millimetres thick and measuring 2.95 by one metre, are an attractive and economical alternative to the blue glass originally projected.

Louafi has inserted the thematic "sluice gates" into the sunken part of the green corridor. The first, between dense rows of trimmed linden trees, is the Patio. Its walls are clad partly with

angezogen – die meisten lassen sich verleiten, sie zu befingern. Solche haptischen Erlebnisse wiederholen sich in den »Schleusen«, Garten-Folies mit einem rauen, erdfarbenen Tierrafino-Putz auf der einen Seite und einem spiegelglatten, blaufarbenen Tadelakputz auf der anderen. Tadelak, ein geölter Kalkputz, ist noch heute in Marokko und in Andalusien gebräuchlich. Am südlichen Ende der Piazza, belegt mit englischen Sandsteinplatten, blicken wir vom Belvedere hinab in die Gärten des Wandels. Unter uns fällt ein drei Meter hoher Wasserfall in ganzer Gartenbreite über eine Edelstahlwanne in ein Becken und schluckt die Geräusche der Expo. Der Wasservorhang hängt vor riesigen, saphirblauen Keramikfliesen aus Megaceran. Diese nur sieben Millimeter dünnen Platten in einer Größe von 2,95 mal einem Meter waren eine reizvolle und kostengünstige Alternative zu dem

Gardens of Change at the Expo 2000 World's Fair in Hannover, Germany
Client: Expo 2000 GmbH
Landscape architect: Kamel Louafi, Berlin
Size: 3.3 hectares
Construction: 1997 – 2000
Costs: DEM 12 million

ursprünglich vorgesehenen, blau gefärbten Glas. Im abgesenkten Teil des Gartenbandes hat Louafi die »Schleusen« als thematische Stationen eingeflochten. Zwischen dichten Reihen geschnittener Linden steht dort zunächst der »Patio«: Seine Wände sind teils mit Lehm, teils mit Tadelak verputzt. In der Mitte spiegelt ein flaches Wasserbecken aus Bollinger Sandstein Himmel, Wolken und bunte Bleiglasvierecke, die in einer pergolaartigen Umrandung aus Zedernholz sitzen.

Vorbei an der Ummantelung aus weißem Lochblech kommen wir ans »Haus der Illusion«, blockiert von einem Kubus aus schwarz durchgefärbtem Glas. Die Künstlichkeit wird gesteigert durch einen Weg aus blauem, mit Edelstahlsplittern versehenen Kunstharz. Wie liegengelassen wirken darin die braunen Ahorn- und Eichenblätter, die unter der Deckschicht aus Epoxyharz liegen.

Auf dem Weg ins »Maschinenhaus« laufen die Lindenreihen aus, begleitet von sechs Klangkörpern aus Edelstahl. Im Maschinenhaus finden sich vier große schwarze Granitblöcke, wie alle anderen bildhauerischen Arbeiten in den Gärten und Parks gearbeitet von den Berliner Steinbildhauern Stefan Sprenker und Thomas Reifferscheid. Zwischen dem »Maschinenhaus« und dem »Teehaus« sorgt ein Wasserspiel für Geräusche und Bewegung. Hier finden sich Bodenplatten aus drei Millimeter starkem Kupfer, die langsam grüngrau werden, sowie ein Wandmosaik aus gebrochenen Megaceranfliesen. Das gleiche Material kennzeichnet den »Wassertisch«: Wasser fließt über den spitz zulaufenden Rand aus Kupferblechen, die mit Schwefelsäure patiniert wurden. Dadurch sehen sie gealtert aus und schimmern nun in vielen Farben durch den Wasserfilm. Im »Teehaus« haben die Bildhauer einen feinkörnigen und farbhomogen roten Sandstein verwendet.

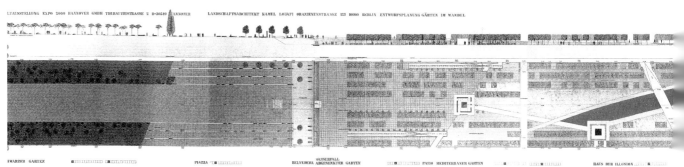

LTAUSSTELLUNG EXPO 2000 HANNOVER GMBH THURNITHISTRASSE 2 D-30519 HANNOVER   LANDSCHAFTSARCHITEKT KAMEL LOUAFI ORANIENSTRASSE 153 10999 BERLIN   ENTWURFSPLANUNG GÄRTEN IM WANDEL

SCHWARZER GARTEN   PIAZZA   BELVEDERE WASSERFALL ABGESENKTER GARTEN   PATIO MEDITERRANER GARTEN   HAUS DER ILLUSION

Als langes Band führen die »Gärten im Wandel« in den Südzipfel des Hannoveraner Expo-Geländes. Im Plan als Farbkonzept angelegt, gewinnt die Abfolge von dunklen zu hellen Räumen erst mit der Materialisierung an Tiefe: Pflanzen, Steine, Holz, Kunststoffe und Licht setzen auf verschiedenen Ebenen das Konzept um.

The Gardens of Change form a long strip extending to the southernmost end of the Expo grounds in Hannover. Conceived in the plan as a colour concept, the progression from dark to light spaces only acquires depth through the materials. Plants, stones, wood, man-made materials, and light realise the concept on many different levels.

Beige verputzte Wände schirmen die Straße ab, durch eine halbtransparente Lattenkonstruktion aus Zedernholz leuchten zwischen dunklen Splittflächen die Bambusbeete, flankiert von weißen und schwarzen Flusskieseln. Richtung »Dünengarten« passieren wir das »Sandhaus«, in dem nordafrikanische Reliefarbeiten die Wände zieren. Über Stege erreichen wir, rechts und links von Strandhafer und Himalaya-Birken (Betula utilis) begleitet, künstliche Dünen aus Einkorn-Beton, abgedeckt mit einer sandfarbenen Polytanschicht.

In einem Obsthain enden die »Gärten im Wandel«. Dahinter beginnt der »Expo-Park-Süd« mit einem großen See, geschwungenen Wegen, wilden Staudenbeeten und orangefarbenen Türmen. Ostwärts erkennt man auf einem Wall sechs Meter hohe Vogelscheuchen aus Rattan, die hinter dem Zaun im »Parc Agricole« erneut auftauchen. Wege aus gebrauchtem Großsteinpflaster und gelber wassergebundener Wegdecke führen durch eine offene Kulturlandschaft mit Solitärbäumen, Strauchgruppen, Einzelsträuchern und Wiesen. In diesem Parkteil wird der grauweiße Kalkmergel des Kronsberges zum Gestaltungsmaterial für Trockenmauern und topographische Reliefs. Mit der Zeit werden diese Elemente zu Kalkmagerrasenstandorten verwittern und damit dem Naturschutz zugute kommen.

Mit seiner lobenswert zurückhaltenden Zeichensprache und seiner mutigen, abwechslungsreichen Materialwahl ist Kamel Louafi der Kultur seines Herkunftslandes Algerien treu geblieben. In allen Details hat er sein Thema beschwingt und spielerisch umgesetzt, nicht mit der Brechstange. Dies leistet nur, wer sich mit den Werkstoffen, Pflanzen inklusive, auskennt, Ungewöhnliches wagt und sich auf risikofreudige Bauherren sowie auf engagierte Bauleiter und Gewerke verlassen kann.

Des Nachts zeichnet Kunstlicht die geometrischen Strukturen der Expo-Gärten nach und verleiht einigen Materialien besonderes Leben, so dem geschwungenen Metallband in der Mitte der Rampe, die zum »Abgesenkten Garten« führt. Das Holz zu beiden Seiten wirkt durch den Kontrast weich wie ein Teppich.

At night artificial light traces the geometric structures of the Expo gardens and makes certain materials come alive, such as the undulating metal band down the middle of the ramp leading to the Sunken Garden. The wood on either side looks as soft as a carpet through the contrast.

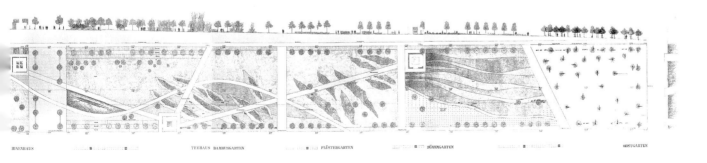

BIENENHAUS   TEEHAUS BAMBUSGARTEN   FLÜSTERGARTEN   DÜNENGARTEN   OBSTGARTEN

Dunkle Diabas-Skulpturen und Vogelscheuchen aus hellem Rattan säumen den Damm im »Expo-Park-Süd«, der zum »Parc Agricole« auf dem Kronsberg führt. Dort werden die Trockenmauern aus anstehendem Kalkmergel mit der Zeit verwittern und die entstehenden Kalkmagerrasen wertvolle Standorte für den Naturschutz abgeben.

Dark diabase sculptures and scarecrows made of pale rattan line the dam in the Expo Park South that leads to the Parc Agricole on the Kronsberg. The dry walls of contiguous limestone marl will eventually deteriorate into chalk grassland that will provide valuable nature conservation sites.

Parc Agricole at the Expo 2000 World's Fair in Hannover, Germany
Client: City of Hannover, Parks Department
Landscape architect: Kamel Louafi, Berlin
Size: 51 hectares (park), 24 hectares (Jardin des Murs, transition areas)
Construction: 1999 – 2000
Costs: DEM 4.7 million

loam and straw and partly with "tadelak." A shallow pool made of Bollingen sandstone in the centre reflects the sky and the clouds as well as the colourful stained glass squares embedded in a pergola-like surround made of cedar.

Past the outer cladding of white perforated sheetmetal, we come to the House of Illusions. Blocking the way is a black-tinted glass cube. Its artificiality is underscored by the blue artificial resin containing high-grade steel chips covering the pathway. Looking like fallen autumn foliage, brown maple and oak leaves are embedded in a top coat of epoxy resin.

The linden rows run out on the way to the Machine House and make way for six fine-steel percussion instruments. In the Machine House are four large black granite blocks carved by the Berlin stone sculptors Stefan Sprenker and Thomas Reifferscheid, who made all the other sculptures in the fair's gardens and parks.

Between the Machine House and the Teahouse, a fountain provides sound and movement. Here we find floor tiles made of copper, three millimetres thick and gradually turning greyish green, as well as a mosaic made of "Megaceran" tile fragments on the wall. Copper also features in the "water table:" water runs over the tapering edge of copper sheets patinated with sulphuric acid to make them age. Their many colours now shimmer through the layer of water.

In the Teahouse the sculptors used red sandstone with a fine grain and homogeneous colour. Beige stucco walls shield the house from the street. Visible through its semitransparent cedar latticework, bamboo beds lined with white and black riverbed gravel sparkle between zones of dark crushed stone.

Proceeding towards the Dune Garden, we pass the Sand House decorated with North African reliefs. Via gangways, with sand reeds and Himalayan birches (*Betula utilis*) on either side, we come to a series of artificial dunes made of concrete (with an aggregate of one size only) coated with a layer of sand-coloured plastic material ("Polytan").

The Gardens of Change end in an orchard. Beyond it extends Expo Park South with its large lake, winding pathways, beds of wild perennials and orange towers. Towards the east you can see six-metre-tall rattan scarecrows on an embankment. They show up again behind a fence in the Parc Agricole.

Pathways paved with large used flagstones and a yellow pavement allowing water runoff lead through an open cultural landscape with single trees, groups of perennials, individual shrubs, and meadows. In this part of the park the grey-white limestone marl of the Kronsberg is the design material used for dry walls and topographical reliefs. These elements will eventually deteriorate into chalk grassland sites and thus serve nature conservation.

In the praiseworthy restraint of his language of forms and the boldness and variety of his choice of materials, Kamel Louafi remained true to his native land of Algeria. That does not only involve traditional materials. Down to the very last detail, the realisation of his theme is lively and playful, never heavy-handed.

This can only be accomplished by someone who knows his way around materials, including plants, who dares to do something unusual, and who can rely on venturesome clients and committed project managers and craftsmen.

Himmelstürme markieren die Südgrenze des »Expo-Parks Süd« und erinnern an die Lehmbauten des algerischen Südens. Im Inneren schaffen blau verputzte Wände eine kühle Atmosphäre im Kontrast zu den sandfarbenen Außenwänden.

Sky-high towers mark the southern limits of the Expo Park South and recall the loam and straw buildings in southern Algeria. The blue stuccoed walls inside create a cool atmosphere in contrast to the sand-coloured exterior.

Expo Park South at the Expo 2000 World's Fair in Hannover, Germany
Client: Expo 2000 GmbH
Landscape architect: Kamel Louafi, Berlin
Size: 17.5 hectares
Construction: 1997 – 2000
Costs: DEM 11 million

Zutphen: Atmosphäre schaffen durch Kontraste

Zutphen: Creating an atmosphere through contrasts

Christ-Jan van Rooij
Martin Knuijt

Alte holländische Städte stehen in enger Verbindung zum Wasser. Dies gilt besonders für die ehemaligen Hansestädte wie Zutphen. Charakteristisch für sie ist der Kontrast zwischen der vom Wall umschlossenen Stadt und dem weiten flachen Umland. Diese Charakteristik spiegelt sich im öffentlichen Raum wider. Verschlungene Straßen und althergebrachte lokale Materialien mischen sich mit dem, was über das Wasser herangeschafft werden konnte. Zahlreiche Gebäude und öffentliche Räume, Weinhaus, Gemüsemarkt, Saatgutmarkt, Holzmarkt und Grafenhof zeugen noch von den mittelalterlichen Aktivitäten. Wie auch in vielen anderen Stadtzentren geriet allmählich die Qualität des öffentlichen Raums immer mehr ins Hintertreffen und der Verschleiß wurde sichtbar.

Qualitativ hochwertige Räume zu schaffen ist ein zeitraubender und langwieriger Prozess. Konsequenz bei der Verwendung von Materialien ist daher von essentieller Bedeutung für die Stadt als Ganzes. Manchmal ist das Material allein nicht genug. Material an sich erzählt keine Geschichte, nur im Zusammenhang und in seinem Kontext erzählt es über die Stadt, den Ort und das Programm. Der Masterplan für die Innenstadt von

Der Masterplan für das Zentrum Zutphens besinnt sich auf die Tradition. Qualitätvolle Materialien sollen den öffentlichen Raum aufwerten.
The master plan for Zutphen reflects a consciousness of tradition. High quality materials are supposed to raise the value of urban open space.

Old Dutch towns are closely connected with water. This goes especially for the former Hanseatic towns like Zutphen. One of its main characteristics is the contrast between the town enclosed by a rampart and its far-reaching flat surroundings. This trait is also reflected in urban open space. Winding streets and old traditional local materials are combined with those which could be brought over on the waterway. Numerous buildings and public places, the wine house, the grocery market, the seed market, the wood market and the count's courtyard are tokens of medieval activities. As with many other town centres the quality of urban open space gradually deteriorated.

To create high quality spaces is a time-consuming and lengthy process. Being consistent concerning the use of materials is, therefore, of essential significance for the town as a whole. Sometimes the material taken by itself is not enough. Material alone does not tell history, but only conveys to us things about a town, a place or a programme in relation to its context. The master plan of the inner town of Zutphen was made to guarantee the unity between design and atmosphere. The new material will remain an integral part of the town for a long time. Material is not the design equipment but the language of a plan. It is an expression of a design conception by the tangible parts of the design. In its essence the material touches upon the innermost being of a conception. Because of the commonly neglectful designing practices concerning urban spaces it is necessary to deal with the material and with details in greater depth. The art of the detail is not the aim of the design, but the translation of a conception into a limited space which finally opens up to the whole. Starting from the conception materials are used which can be derived from that conception. Sand, wood, metal ore, stone, gravel, trees and loam are converted into concrete, terrazzo, cut polyester concrete, glass, glued wood, sealing material, high-grade steel, blocks of natural rock, epoxy resin, rubber and bricks. The materials are in a technical sense transformed and manipulated to the limiting point of their feasible applications. In Zutphen steel is used in contrast to the traditional pavements. It shoots up from the ground, so to speak, and bends itself to an object to sit on. Other materials are chosen because they catch the light, and can refract it into contrasts or into nuances of a certain colour spectrum. An often used contrast is light and dark. In Zutphen you can easily observe how materials react to changed conditions. Materials absorb the weather conditions. Whenever it rains stones become darker, and start to shine, in the sun they turn white. The colour spectrum of the lit up shopping windows is reflected by the paved surface. The material adopts the colour of its surroundings, and becomes an integral part of it.

In the evenings the lights enhance the medieval atmosphere of the buildings. Gentle light shines on the roof ledges and the brick facades. It is this indirect lighting that spreads a velvet fairy-tale-like gleam over the town without revealing the light sources within one's view of the street. Contrasts in material and light produce an exciting view. Especially in northern Europe, where the skies are often overcast and where it rains often, they are especially effective. The strongest contrasts, like black and white, rough and fine textures, dull and shiny materials create a sense of

Zutphen wurde erstellt, um die Einheit von Entwurf und Atmosphäre zu gewährleisten. Das neue Material wird über lange Zeit hinweg Bestandteil der Stadt bleiben. Material ist nicht die Ausstattung, sondern die Sprache eines Entwurfs. Es ist der Ausdruck des Entwurfskonzepts in fassbaren Bestandteilen. Material berührt in seiner Essenz das tiefste Wesen des Konzepts. Wegen der oft nachlässigen Gestaltung der Stadträume ist es notwendig, sich intensiv mit Material und Details zu befassen.

Die Kunst des Details ist nicht Entwurfsziel, sondern die Übersetzung des Konzepts in einen Raum, der schließlich aufgeht im Ganzen. Ausgehend vom Konzept werden Materialien verwendet, die man herleiten kann. Sand, Holz, Erz, Stein, Schotter, Bäume und Lehm werden zu Beton, Terrazzo, geschliffenem Polyesterbeton, Glas, Leimholz, Schiffshaut, Edelstahl, Natursteinblöcken, Epoxidharz, Gummi und Backstein. Die Materialien werden in technischem Sinn bis an die Grenze ihrer Anwendungsmöglichkeiten transformiert und manipuliert. In Zutphen wird der Stahl als Kontrast zu den traditionellen Bodenbelägen verwendet. Er schießt aus dem Grund und biegt sich zu einem Sitzobjekt. Andere Materialien werden gewählt, weil sie Licht einfangen und zu Kontrasten oder aber zu Nuancen eines bestimmten Farbspektrums brechen können. Ein häufig genutzer

Der Masterplan sieht qualitätvolle Materialien für die Innenstadt von Zutphen vor: Roter holländischer Klinkerstein und Steinbänder aus belgischem Blaustein ergänzen sich spannungsvoll in der Langen Hofstraat.

The master plan has designed high-quality materials for the town centre of Zutphen: Red Dutch bricks and strips of Belgian blue stone complement each other in a scintillating manner in the Langen Hofstraat.

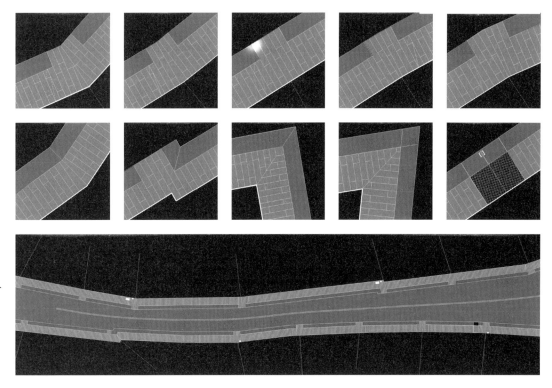

Kontrast ist hell-dunkel. In Zutphen lässt sich gut verfolgen, wie Material auf veränderte Bedingungen reagiert. Materialien absorbieren die Witterung. Wenn es regnet, wird der Stein dunkler und beginnt zu glänzen, bei Sonne ist er weiß. Das Farbspektrum der erleuchteten Schaufenster spiegelt sich im Straßenbelag wider. Das Material absorbiert die Farbe seiner Umgebung und wird zu deren Bestandteil.

Abends unterstreicht die Beleuchtung die Atmosphäre der mittelalterlichen Gebäude. Sanftes Licht strahlt auf Dachgesimse und Backsteinfassaden. Es ist diese indirekte Beleuchtung, die einen samtenen märchenhaften Schimmer über die Stadt breitet, ohne dass die Lichtquellen im Straßenbild zu sehen wären. Kontraste in Material und Licht erzeugen ein spannendes Bild. Gerade im Norden Europas, wo der Himmel oft bedeckt ist, und es viel regnet, sind sie besonders wirkungsvoll. Die stärksten Kontraste, wie schwarz-weiß, grobe und feine Texturen, matte und glänzende Materialien, schaffen Räumlichkeit. Das Glitzern des Regens, der Widerschein von Licht und der Schattenfall, Textur und Fühlbarkeit, raue und glatte Materialien werden erfahrbar in den Straßen.

spaciousness. The shimmering of the rain, the bright reflections of light, the outlines of the shadows, texture and perceptibility, rough and smooth materials are especially susceptible to experience in the streets. Urban space within the Zutphen town centre is gradually changing. What is so beautiful about the Dutch town is that it forms a unity between scale and material, but can at the same time be very rich in the variations of form. The shopping centre of Zutphen is provided with streets paved with bricks and a modern variant of sidewalks. The market places are laid out with surfaces of natural stone throughout the area, and designed with asymmetrically arranged sidewalks. The 's Gravenhof square around which the administration centre has always been concentrated is turned into a paved

area of natural rock with footpaths for the important buildings which in turn determine their position. The Lange Hofstraat forms the most important connection between the administration centre and the market places. It constitutes, so to speak, a brace between two main focuses of interest. The character of the squares paved with monumental natural rock is continued along the Lange Hofstraat by matching the stone paving in the market places. Broad, blue strips of stone pavement accentuate the bends of the street.

The transformation of the town centre of Zutphen is very gradually taking form. The finished areas provide an inspiring incentive for the projects to come. Meanwhile, the blueprints for the market places and town squares are already in their advanced stages.

Der öffentliche Raum in der Zutphener Innenstadt verändert sich langsam aber stetig. Das Schöne an der alten holländischen Stadt ist, dass sie in Maßstab und Material eine Einheit bildet, in der Form aber sehr abwechslungsreich sein kann. Das Einkaufszentrum erhält Straßen mit Backsteinpflaster und einer modernen Variante der Gehwege, die Marktplätze bekommen ein Natursteinpflaster über die volle Breite sowie asymmetrisch angeordnete Bürgersteige. Der Platz 's Gravenhof, um den sich seit jeher das Verwaltungszentrum konzentriert, wird zu einem Natursteinplatz mit Gehwegen für die wichtigen Gebäude. Zwischen dem Verwaltungszentrum und den Marktplätzen stellt die Lange Hofstraat die wichtigste Verbindung dar. Sie ist die Klammer zwischen zwei Schwerpunkten. Der Charakter der mit Naturstein gepflasterten Plätze setzt sich in der Lange Hofstraat fort in einer zum monumentalen Pflaster passenden Pflasterung der Märkte. Breite blaue Steinbänder begleiten die Krümmung der Straße. Ganz allmählich nimmt der Umbau der Zutphener Innenstadt Gestalt an. Die fertiggestellten Bereiche geben den Anstoß für die folgenden Projekte. Inzwischen sind die Entwürfe für die Marktplätze und Stadtplätze weit fortgeschritten.

Renewal of the open urban space in Zutphen, The Netherlands
Client: City of Zutphen
Landscape architects: Okra, Utrecht (project architects: Christ-Jan van Rooij, Martin Knuijt, Boudewijn Almekinders)
Planning team: Koen Schrauwen, landscape architect; Mirjam Jansen, technical engineer; Amal Kafu, architectural designer
Size: 32 hectares in the historical centre of Zutphen
Planning: 1997 – 1999 (master plan), 1997 – 2003 detailed plans
Construction: 1998 – 2004
Costs: NGL 10.55 million for the first four stages

London: Backstein und Farbflächen

London: Bricks and coloured surfaces

Johanna Gibbons

In London gibt es einen Ort, der durch die Jahrhunderte hindurch ein Brennpunkt bedeutender geschichtlicher Ereignisse war: der Edward Platz im Viertel Islington. Trotz seiner historischen Bedeutung stellte sich der Platz zunächst als Leere dar. Eine Gruppe aus Aktivisten, Mitgliedern des lokalen Forums und der örtlichen Gemeindeverwaltung war mit der Bitte an uns herangetreten, die Gemeinde bei der Umgestaltung des Platzes zu beraten; so sollten insbesondere die wesentlichen Anliegen der Bewohner ermittelt und darauf aufbauend ein Entwurf vorbereitet sowie ein Gebot für die Realisierung des Projektes abgegeben werden. Die kontinuierliche Zusammenarbeit mit einer eigens eingerichteten Projektsteuerungsgruppe und zweier benachbarter Schulen stellte die erfolgreiche Umsetzung unseres Planes sicher.

Unser Entwurf für den Edward Platz gliedert sich in drei Bereiche: eine Aktivzone, die als Blumenwiese auf beiden Seiten eines über die Jahre hinweg ausgetretenen Fußweges entlang einer Durchgangsstraße angelegt wird; ein kleiner obstbaumbestandener Eingangsbereich sowie eine naturnahe und ursprüngliche Wildblumen-

Auf den Fundamenten eines zerstörten Backsteinhauses aus dem 19. Jahrhundert entstand im Viertel Islington ein kleiner Park.

Upon the foundations of a destroyed 19th century brick house in the district of Islington a small park emerged.

Edward Square is a place at a point of convergence with a background of many notable historical events throughout the ages. At first the square presented itself as a void charged with significance, however, flat and featureless. We were asked by a community group of campaign activists and members of the local forum and the local authorities to counsel the community, to establish their needs and priorities and to prepare a design as well as a bid for funding. The success of the bid was largely due to the thoroughness and depth of the consultations achieved. Persistent collaboration with the Steering Group and the two local schools ensured that a continuous dialogue was maintained throughout the construction phase.

The plan consists of three sections – an activity section on a flowery lawn on either side of a well-trodden thoroughfare footpath, a small orchard entrance area and a meadow with a wide range of native wild flowers. The park is supposed to encapsulate the complex aspirations of an inner city community by means of a steadily ongoing process of cooperation and design.

The project is geared towards integrating traces of the past with present day needs. It is intended to serve as an educational resource for the neighbouring schools, as a festival site and as a retreat for quiet day-dreaming. The selection of materials and the detailed planning and design grew out of an in-depth understanding of the site. Site investigations revealed piles of bricks and building foundations dating back to 1853. The line of seating plinths using recycled bricks corresponds to the back line of the terrace reminding us of the architecture which formerly surrounded the square. The plinths are made of lightly shaded, generously arranged one by one metre square table top seating units located within a bosque of honey locust trees, and are surrounded by steel frames supporting green roofs of Russian vine.

The original cobbled lane of Mount Sorrel granite was another special feature of the site. Despite its unevenness the surface was not re-laid, so for the most part the undulations remain to be seen as evidence of former times, and have only been levelled out at the gateways. In the main square slabs using the same kind of granite composition are banded together with a ground and textured finish. Within the orchard and along the fringe bordering the nature area they are turf-jointed and plug-planted with rosemary, thyme, lavender and sage.

The collaboration with artist Kate Blee was concerned with transforming an imposing blank wall, and has resulted in creating an interactive surface conducive to ball games.

Pure mineral colours were selected in view of colour density and vibrancy, and were painted in

wiese. Der Park ist so konzipiert, dass seine Nutzung nicht zwingend vorgeschrieben ist. Mit Hilfe eines kontinuierlichen Austausches zwischen allen Beteiligten sollen die vielschichtigen Erwartungen und Hoffnungen einer innerstädtischen Gemeinde, die an die Umgestaltung des Platzes geknüpft sind, zusammengefasst und integriert werden. So soll der Park einmal nicht nur als eine Art Bildungseinrichtung für die beiden in der Nähe liegenden Schulen genutzt werden, sondern auch als Veranstaltungsort oder als Rückzugsgebiet für leise Tagträume.

Die Auswahl der Materialien nimmt Rücksicht auf die Geschichte des Ortes. Untersuchungen brachten Fundamente eines zerstörten Backsteinhauses aus dem Jahre 1853 zum Vorschein. Heute grenzen Sitzgelegenheiten aus recycelten Ziegelsteinen direkt an die Stelle, an der einmal die Terrasse dieses Hauses lag und erinnern uns an das Gebäude. Die Sitzelemente sind aus leicht nuancierten, ein mal ein Meter großen Tischplatten gefertigt, die in einem Boskett aus Gleditsien großzügig angeordnet sind. Russischer Wein lässt mit Hilfe von Stahlrahmen grüne Dächer über die Sitzelemente wachsen.

Der Platz wies noch eine weitere Besonderheit auf: eine Durchgangsstraße aus Granitkopfsteinpflaster (Mount Sorrel Granit). Trotz der Unebenheiten wurden die Pflastersteine nicht neu verlegt; das Auf und Ab blieb so zum größten Teil erhalten und ist heute ein Zeugnis vergangener Tage. Nur an den Zufahrten und Zugängen des Parks wurde das Pflaster nivelliert. In der Mitte des Platzes wurden Platten aus derselben Granitzusammensetzung verlegt und mit einem strukturierten Abschluss versehen: Innerhalb des Obstgartens und entlang der Trennlinie zwischen dem naturnahen Bereich auf der einen und dem versiegelten Platz auf der anderen Seite wurden sie auf Lücke verlegt. Die so entstandenen Zwischenräume wurden mit Gras und punktuell mit Rosmarin, Thymian, Lavendel und Salbei bepflanzt. Die Umgestaltung einer imposanten leeren Mauer wurde der Künstlerin Kate Blee übertragen. Sie schuf daraus eine interaktive

Vor kurzem noch ungemütlich und leer, bietet der umgestaltete Edward-Platz im Londoner Stadtteil Islington heute Raum für individuelle und gemeinschaftliche Nutzungen. Zahlreiche Sitzelemente bereichern den Platz, für ein Sitzelement aus Beton verfasste der Dichter Andrew Motion ein Gedicht, von Gary Breeze künstlerisch umgesetzt.

Previously uncomfortable and empty, Edward Square now provides space for individual and common uses in the London district of Islington. Numerous seating elements enhance the square. The poet Andrew Motion wrote a poem for a concrete seating element which was artfully cast by Gary Breeze.

ATH US NOW IT GLEAMS OFF ROMANS FACING BOAD FLOWS OVER CHARTISTS ON THEIR PICKS UP A RAILWAY TREMOR IN A TERRACE ROW THEN LEAPS TO HOLD A JUMP-JET IN THIN AIR

OF FREEDOM LEARNING HOW TO FIND ITS AIM TO PROVE OUR LIVES OUR OWN YOU'VE YOURS, I'VE MINE EACH ONE DIFFERENT BUT EACH THE SAME

Oberfläche, die für Ballspiele geeignet ist. Für die Gestaltung der Mauer wählte die Künstlerin reine mineralische Farben aus – sie zeichnen sich insbesondere durch hohe Farbdichte und Farbdynamik aus. Die Farben wurden in eckigen Formen und gleichmäßigen Farbmustern aufgetragen – als Gegensatz zu den organischen Landschaftsmustern des Parks.

Dort, wo früher das Backsteinhaus stand, wachsen nun Bäume. Eine Gruppe von Platanen (Plantanus x acerifolia) bildet hier die Grenze des Parks. Aufgrund ihrer unterschiedlichen Größe und Anordnung stellen sie einen deutlichen Kontrast zu den als Boskett angeordneten Gleditsien (Gleditsia triacanthos 'Inermis') dar. Das Blattwerk der Gleditsien lässt unschöne Ausblicke verschwinden und spendet einen lichten strukturierten Schatten. Zwei große Eichen (Quercus robur) locken zahlreiche Tierarten in den Park und ein Obsthain aus drei verschiedenen Arten von zierenden Holzapfelbäumen (Malus 'Everest', 'Professor Sprenger', 'Makamik') umgeben einen bereits vorhandenen und vielgeliebten Apfelbaum. Die halb ausgewachsene Trauerweide (Salix x alba 'tristis') wird eines Tages möglicherweise ein grünes Eingangstor in den Park bilden.

Verschiedene Sitzelemente bereichern den Platz. So bieten Stufen im Rasen größeren Schulklassen oder Zuschauergruppen während einer Veranstaltung Platz. Kleinere Gruppen oder Einzelpersonen finden Abgeschiedenheit und Schutz auf den Ziegel- und Holzsockeln im Boskett. Im Obsthain auf der anderen Seite wurden einzelne Sitzelemente aufgestellt, die besonders für Gruppen geeignet sind. Für Mütter mit Kindern gibt es niedrige Bänke aus Holz und Gusseisen. Darüber hinaus wurden um eine der beiden Eichen herum einige Steine angeordnet, die für kleine Schulklassen etwas Sitzfläche bieten. Diese können beispielsweise auch als Trittsteine genutzt oder als Inseln gesehen werden. Eisbergen gleich, scheint ihr in der Erde enthaltener Umfang ein Geheimnis zu bergen. Ihre Formen und Strukturen erzählen Geschichten aus vergangenen geologischen Zeitaltern, von Prozessen und Metamorphosen. Die körnige Struktur der Steine macht deutlich, welch starke natürliche Kräfte notwendig sind, um Schlamm und Sand in Stein zu verwandeln.

angular forms with regular patches of colour in order to present a contrast to the organic landscape patterns of the park.

Trees create an enclosure around the area where the buildings used to be. An alignment of London planes (Plantanus x acerifolia) form the edge of the park.

Due to their difference in size and in the density of their arrangement they present a clear contrast to the bosque of honey locust trees (Gleditsia triacanthos 'Inermis') which screen off un-

Kräftige Farben und eckige Formen wählte die Künstlerin Kate Blee für die Ballspielwand. Stahlrahmen, bewachsen mit Russischem Wein, bilden künftig ein grünes Dach über den Sitzelementen. Deren Sitzflächen bestehen aus ein mal ein Meter großen Tischplatten, die recycelten Ziegelsteine erinnern an ein früheres Backsteinhaus.

The artist Kate Blee chose strong colours and angular forms for the ball playing wall. Steel frames covered with Russian grape vine will eventually form a green roof over the seating elements. Their seating surfaces consist of one by one metre large table plates. The recycled bricks remind one of a former brick house.

sightly views and provide a finely textured, dappled shade. Two large oaks (*Quercus robur*) are apt to encourage wildlife into the park, and an orchard of three types of ornamental crab apple trees (*Malus 'Everest', 'Professor Sprenger', 'Makamik'*) encircle an already existing well-loved apple tree.

The semi-mature weeping willow (*Salix alba 'tristis'*) will eventually form a green gateway to the park.

Seating accommodation has been designed as an integral part of the park. There are ample step sitting opportunities around the south of the lawn capable of accommodating large school parties or spectator groups during a festival.

Small groups or individuals can easily find seclusion and shelter on the brick and timber plinths within the bosque. In the orchard on the other hand individual seats have been arranged for group settings.

Low bench seating made of timber and cast iron has been provided for mothers with children of different ages. The benches have been positioned centrally in the park, thus enabling easy surveillance and offering plenty of room for prams and bikes without having them block the thoroughfare.

Then there are rocks providing seats for small classes of pupils around an oak tree. These may also serve as stepping stones, or can be seen as "islands". Like icebergs, their volume submerged below the ground seems to pose a mystery. Their forms and textures tell tales of geological times, processes and layers of metamorphoses. The grain textures of the rocks are tokens of the powerful natural forces which are necessary to turn mud and sand into stone.

In drei Bereiche gliedert sich der Edward-Platz: eine Blumenwiese beidseits des Fußweges, einen obstbaumbestandenen Eingangsbereich und eine naturnahe Wildblumenwiese. In der Mitte des Platzes wurden Granitplatten verlegt, teils auf Lücke, bepflanzt mit Gras, Rosmarin, Lavendel und Salbei.

Edward Square is divided into three areas: A flowery meadow on both sides of the foot path, an orchard in the entrance area, and a nature-like wildflower meadow. Granite plates were laid out in the centre of the square, partly with gaps planted with grass, rosemary, lavender and sage.

Edward Square, Islington, London, Great Britain
Client: London Borough of Islington with the Edward Square Steering Group
Funding: Kings Cross Partnership
Design and public consultation: J & L Gibbons, landscape architects (Johanna Gibbons, David Chanter, Charlie Voss, Karen Lacey, Neil Davidson)
Artists: Kate Blee (panel), Andrew Motion (poem), Gary Breeze (lettering)
Size: 0.5 hectares
Planning: 1997 – 1999
Construction: 1999 – 2000
Costs: GBP 301,000

Schweden: die Farbe Grau

Sweden: The colour grey

Bengt Isling

Ich besitze zwei Anzüge. Den einen hatte ich 1973 voller Stolz gekauft, als ich mich an der Universität Ultuna einschrieb. Es war ein gelbbrauner Baumwollgabardine-Anzug, auf Figur geschnitten und mit bemerkenswert breiten Aufschlägen. Leider nützte er mir gar nichts in den Anfangs-Semestern meines Landschaftsarchitekturstudiums. Da waren schon die Gummistiefel angemessener, die ich mir bereits in der ersten Woche kaufen musste. Mein zweiter Anzug ist dunkelgrau. Ich habe ihn dieses Frühjahr gekauft, für die Eröffnung der Bibliothek in Linköping. Mit einem grauen Anzug ist man überall richtig gekleidet, zum Beispiel, wenn man den König, die Königin oder einen Minister trifft – was der Fall war. Grau ist die Farbe des »Normalen«.

Irgendwie ist es die langweiligste Farbe überhaupt. Der Straßenstaub an den Schuhen und die Staubballen unter dem Bett sind grau. Mischen Sie alle Farben in Ihrem Farbkasten, und Sie bekommen Grau. Kein Wunder, dass man vom grauen Alltag spricht. Grau wie das Haar der Alten, grau wie der Nebel. Und doch – graue Schläfen oder eine nebelverhangene Küste können wunderschön sein.

In meiner Heimat ist der Boden oft grau. Das liegt am anstehenden Gestein Schwedens. Granit und Gneis sind grau, obwohl sie freilich verschieden viele rote, weiße und schwarze mineralische Bestandteile enthalten. Wie in Aquarellen verschwimmen diese Farben zu Grau – und das ergibt den grauen Schotter, der als Bodenbelag und Zuschlagstoff zum Beton diesem die »natürliche« Farbe Grau gibt. Schmutz und Staub lassen nach einigen Jahren schließlich auch den Asphalt ergrauen.

Grau ist nie falsch, kann aber langweilen. Details verleihen grauen Anzügen, grauen Schläfen oder grauem Fels etwas Atemberaubendes. Grey is never wrong but it can be boring. It takes details to turn grey suits, grey hair or grey stone into something breathtaking.

I have owned two suits. The first I proudly bought for my matriculation in 1973. It was a brown ochre cotton gabardine suit, very tight and with memorable wide lapels. Unfortunately, it did not turn out to be very useful when I began my studies in landscape architecture at Ultuna. The rubber boots I had to purchase by my first

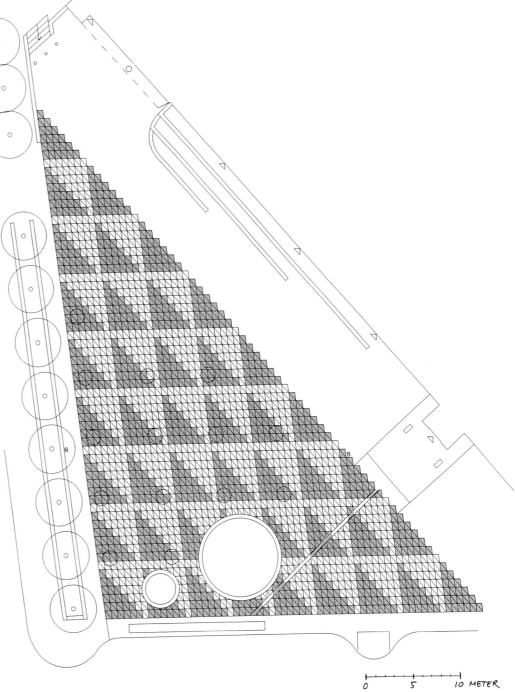

0   5   10 METER

week there were much more appropriate. The second suit of mine is dark grey. I bought it for the inauguration of the Linköping Public Library this spring. Wear a grey suit and you are always presentable. You can wear it to meet the king, the queen or the minister. And I did. Grey is the colour of normality. In some way grey is the dullest of all colours. The dirt on your soles and the dust balls under your bed are grey. If you mix all the paints in your box of watercolours you end up with grey. Similarly, if boring everyday life had a colour it must be grey. Grey as old hair. Grey as fog. Nevertheless, both aged hair and foggy coastlines can be seen as beautiful and promising, instead of merely dull. Where I live the ground surfaces are often grey. This is due to the bedrock, which is basically grey in Sweden. The granite and gneiss are usually grey, mixed with more or less red, white and black minerals. These colours blend to form grey the way the watercolours do. This is why the gravel on the ground is grey. Concrete contains gravel as ballast; hence grey is its natural colour. Asphalt also becomes grey over the years, from the dirt and dust accumulating on the surface. There are of course materials in other colours on the ground. Red or yellow brick are obvious examples. Differently coloured imported gravel is used as a surface or as ballast in concrete. The bedrock also contains red granite, limestone, sandstone and black diabases, to mention only a few. For the museum of Värmland in Karlstad, for instance, we used a clear blue cyanite from a quarry in the region. Nowadays manufacturers of concrete paving can deliver almost any colour desired. Yet even these materials have an observable tendency to become grey with age and dirt. The colours seem somewhat superfluous.

Natürlich gibt es auch andersfarbige Bodenbeläge. Roter oder gelber Klinker fallen einem ein. Importierter Schotter wird als Bodenbelag benutzt oder dem Beton hinzugefügt. Es gibt auch roten Granit als Grundgestein, oder Kalkstein, Sandstein und schwarzen Diabas, um nur einige zu nennen. Im Värmland-Museum in Karlstad haben wir leuchtend blauen Cyanit aus einem Steinbruch in der Umgebung eingesetzt. Die Hersteller von Pflasterbelägen können heutzutage fast jede gewünschte Farbe liefern.

Grau, der unbunten Farbe zwischen weiß und schwarz, haftet etwas Langweiliges an und doch ist sie zugleich die Farbe der Geister. Für den Bibliotheksplatz in Linköping verwendeten die Landschaftsarchitekten Schotter, Stein, Granit, Beton, Aluminium und Stahl – alles in Grau.

Grey, that not colourful colour between white and black, has something boring about even though it is also the colour of ghosts. For the Library Square in Linköping the landscape architects used crushed rock, stone, granite, concrete, aluminium and steel – all in grey, light here and dark there.

Alle Farben aber haben deutlich die Tendenz, durch Alter und Schmutz grau zu werden. Vielleicht sind sie auch ein bisschen überflüssig.

In Linköping haben wir das Grau in seiner Tiefe ausgelotet. Der anstehende Fels ist grau. Wir haben Schotter, Stein, Granit, Beton, Aluminium und Stahl verwendet. Das Grau ist entweder dunkel oder hell, die eingeschlossenen Mineralien fügen eine Menge Farben hinzu. Das Grau wird zum kühlen Hintergrund für die Menschen und die Pflanzen.

In Linköping we explored grey in some depth. We used gravel, stone, granite, concrete, aluminium and steel. The regional bedrock is grey. It is either dark or light and contains a lot of colours in the minerals. The grey forms a cool background for both the people and the vegetation.

Grey paving. The triangular Library Square fills the space between the library and the surrounding buildings. The triangular shape is emphasised by the planted ash trees and by concrete paving especially designed for the site. It consists of rhomboid tiles in two colours: grey and dark grey.

Granite paving stone. The granite paving is quarried in northern Skåne. It is warm grey with pale red and pink stripes. The same granite is used for the walls around the preserved elm trees. Rubble stones are used in the narrow ditch, framed with steel, which drains the rainwater runoff from the roof of the building along the park facade.

Grey planters. On the eastern side of the building is an area facing the medieval castle. Here we placed four planters of cast aluminium. The colour of the planters is – you guessed it – grey.

Grey steel. In front of the building is a parterre of beech hedges. They are trimmed to form letters. Around the letters is a border of grey galvanised steel. The colour scheme could be a parody of Henry Ford's statement, changing it to: "You can get any colour you like as long as it is grey."

Graues Pflaster. Der dreieckige, multifunktionale Bibliotheksvorplatz leitet seine Form aus der Anordnung der Bibliothek und der umgebenden Gebäude ab.

Hier geht man zum Haupteingang, hier stehen der Bibliotheksbus, Fahrräder, Autos und ein Café. Die Dreiecksform wird durch die Eschen am Rande und ein eigens entworfenes Betonpflaster betont. Rhombenförmige Platten fügen sich zu einem Bodenmuster in zwei Farben: hellgrau und dunkelgrau.

Grauer Stein. Pflastersteine und Stufen aus Granit umgeben das Betonpflaster. Der Granit kommt aus Nord-Schonen und hat einen warmen Grauton mit blassroten und rosa Streifen. Denselben Granit verwendeten wir für die Einfassungen der Ulmen. Die schmale, stahlbandgefasste Traufrinne vor der Fassade zum Park hin gestalteten wir mit Kieselsteinen.

Graue Pflanzgefäße. Vier Pflanzgefäße aus Aluminium stehen zwischen der Bibliothek und der mittelalterlichen Burg von Linköping. Ihre Farbe ist – Sie ahnen es schon – grau.

Grauer Stahl. Vor dem Gebäude, zum Park hin, befindet sich ein Parterre aus Buchenhecken, geschnitten in Buchstaben-Formen. Wir haben jene Buchstaben gewählt, die interessante Räume ergeben. Eingefasst wurden sie mit grauem galvanisierten Stahl.

Das ganze Farbenspiel könnte glatt als Variante des Spruches von Henry Ford durchgehen: »Sie können jede beliebige Farbe wählen – Hauptsache, sie ist grau«.

Grau als kühler Hintergrund für Menschen und Pflanzen: Rhombenförmige Betonplatten in hell- und dunkelgrau, eingefasst von Pflastersteinen aus Granit, Fahrradständer aus Beton, Bänke aus Stein.

Grey forms a cool background for people and plants: rhomboid concrete tiles in light and dark grey are surrounded by granite paving stones, concrete bicycle racks and stone benches.

Municipal library, Linköping, Sweden
Client: City of Linköping
Landscape architects: Bengt Isling (responsible) and Nina Medén, Nyréns arkitektkontor, Stockholm
Architects: Johan Nyrén and collaborators, Nyréns arkitektkontor, Stockholm
Size: 7,000 square meters
Competition: 1997
Planning 1998 – 1999
Construction: 1999 – 2000
Costs: SEK 5.4 million

Holland: Hardware versus Software

Holland: Hardware versus software

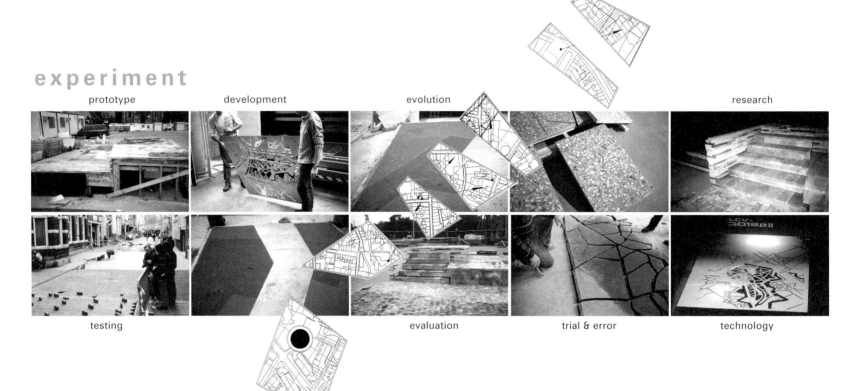

experiment

prototype   development   evolution   research

testing   evaluation   trial & error   technology

Bart Brands
Karel Loeff

Materialien und Entwurf bedingen sich gegenseitig. Ein Plädoyer für interaktives Entwickeln von Zielen, Räumen und Materialien.

Materials and design are contingent on each other. The authors appeal for an interactive development of aims, spaces and materials.

Beim Planen öffentlicher Räume ist die Auswahl der Materialien leider viel zu oft vom Entwurfsprozess losgelöst. So kommt es nicht selten vor, dass die Planer mit traditionellen Raumkonzepten die Illusion innovativer Lösungen erwecken, indem sie allein neue Materialien einsetzen, die dann jedoch nichts weiter sind als eine dünne, modische Schicht, die Erneuerung suggeriert.

Statisch versus dynamisch. In unserem Büro herrscht die Auffassung, dass der Materialeinsatz integraler Bestandteil des Entwurfsprozesses sein sollte. Die Materialien, die »Hardware« eines Projekts, verleihen dem Entwurf oft etwas Endgültiges, wenig Flexibles, und ihre Auswahl fällt solange schwer, wie es keine »Software« gibt, die einem die Entscheidungskriterien liefert. Darum hängt der Erfolg eines Projektes sehr stark vom Entwurfskonzept und noch viel mehr vom Entwurfsverlauf ab. Kontext, Funktion und Evolution im Laufe der Zeit bilden zusammen allmählich ein Grundprogramm für den zu bauenden Raum.

Leider wird das Entwerfen von Parks und anderen öffentlichen Stadträumen immer öfter

In planning public spaces, the choice of materials is unfortunately all too often made outside of the design process. It is hence not unusual for planners to create an illusion of innovative solutions in traditional spatial concepts simply by using new materials. These are thus no more than a thin fashionable veneer that suggests novelty.

Static versus dynamic. In our office we believe that the application of materials should be an integral part of the design process. The materials, the "hardware" of a project, lend a design something final that is not very flexible. Their selection is difficult as long as there is no "software" to provide criteria for decision-making. That is why the success of a project depends a lot on the design concept and even more on the design process. In the course of time, the context, function and evolution combine to form a basic programme. Unfortunately, the design of parks and other public spaces is becoming increasingly

detailing

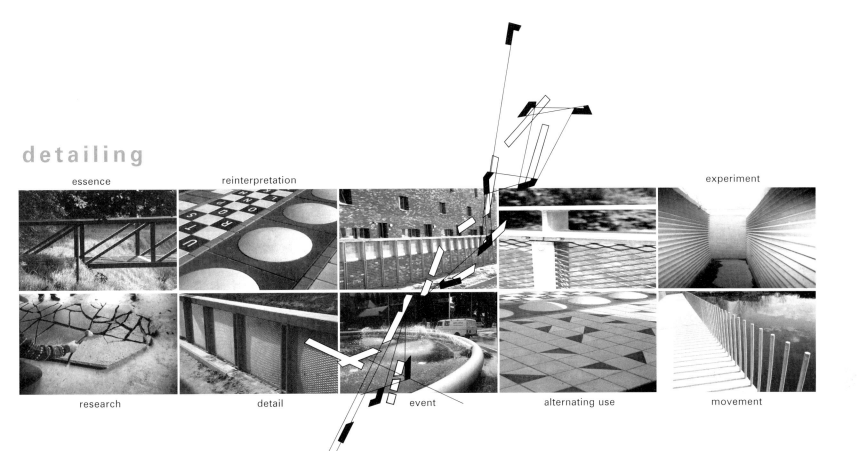

essence   reinterpretation   experiment

research   detail   event   alternating use   movement

equated with architectural design. This gives the design a static character. In accordance with the space framework and the budget concerned, the landscape architect delivers a design, and subsequently works out the construction plans from which construction proceeds. The job is done. There is no room left for thought, experiments and developments.

The time factor. For centuries, however, time was the landscape architect's most important tool. By a fixed deadline, the planner and client were able to have an impression of the picture desired, and a work schedule listed the objectives still to be met. There was scope for revisions based on economic, natural, social and cultural changes. The contours of a project were established but adjustments were welcome. We believe that this procedure should be revived. We were pleased to note many a client actually supports this culture of planning. The definition of public

dem architektonischen Gestalten gleichgesetzt. Das verleiht dem Entwurf einen statischen Charakter. Abgestimmt auf einen räumlichen Rahmen und ein Budget liefert der Landschaftsarchitekt den Entwurf mit allen Details ab und arbeitet anschließend die Werkpläne aus, nach denen gebaut wird. Damit hat er seine Aufgabe erfüllt. Für Nachdenken, Experimente und Weiterentwicklung bleibt ihm in den meisten Fällen kein Spielraum.

Der Faktor Zeit. Jahrhundertelang war jedoch die Zeit das wichtigste Instrument des Landschaftsarchitekten. Zur einer festgesetzten Frist konnten Landschaftsarchitekten und Bauherren sich einen Eindruck vom gewünschten Bild verschaffen, und ein Ablaufplan gab die Ziele an, die noch zu erreichen waren.

Es blieb Raum für Korrekturen aufgrund ökonomischer, natürlicher, sozialer und kultureller Veränderungen. Die Konturen des Projektes standen fest, aber Anpassungen waren willkommen. Unserer Meinung nach sollte dieser Prozess wieder aufgegriffen werden. Erfreut stellen wir fest, dass mancher Auftraggeber diese Planungskultur unterstützt.

Obgleich sich die Bedeutung des Öffentlichen in einer Zeit der digitalen Netzwerke, des Cyberspace und der Datenautobahnen ändert, bleibt der physische öffentliche Raum der einzige wirkliche Treffpunkt für die

Experimentelles Erproben der »Hardware«, also der Materialien eines Projektes, hilft den Planern des Büros Karres en Brands zu entscheiden, wie sie ihre Entwürfe materialisieren. In Bergen-op-Zoom bauten sie den Gouvernementsplein während der Ausführungsplanung und entwickelten zusammen mit Bauherr, Konstrukteuren und Baufirmen neue Techniken für den Materialeinsatz.

Experimental testing of "hardware," i.e. materials for a project, helps the planners of the Karres en Brands office to decide how to make their designs materialise. In Bergen-op-Zoom they built the Gouvernementsplein while the realisation planning was in progress and, in collaboration with the client, builders and construction companies, they developed new techniques for using materials.

is undergoing change in a time of digital networks, cyberspace and data super highways. Nevertheless, physical public space remains the only true place for people to meet, albeit in increasingly subdivided groups. It provides room for communication and is vital for giving people a feeling of being rooted. That is why it is so important not to squeeze public spaces into a design

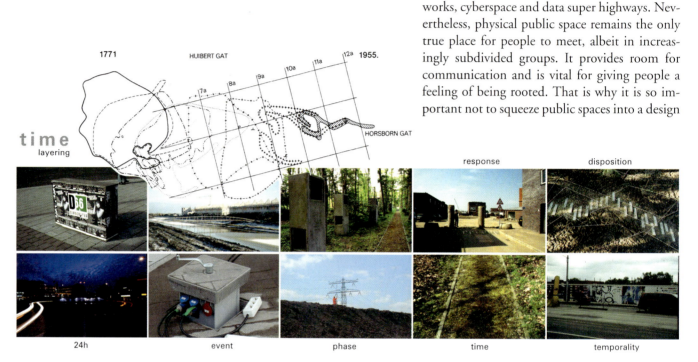

time layering

response   disposition

24h   event   phase   time   temporality

Menschen, wenn auch mehr und mehr nach Gruppen sortiert. Er bietet Raum für Austausch und ist gleichzeitig von vitaler Bedeutung für die Verwurzelung der Menschen, für das Gefühl, am richtigen Platz Teil eines größeren Ganzen zu sein.

Daher ist es wichtig, öffentliche Orte nicht in ein gestalterisches Korsett zu zwängen, sondern sie so anzulegen, dass sie sich den immer schneller wandelnden Gewohnheiten, Wünschen und Bedürfnissen der Nutzer anpassen können.

Neue Schichten im Ökosystem. Wir betrachten den öffentlichen Raum als subtiles Ökosystem. Kein natürliches, sondern ein abstraktes Netz sich einander beeinflussender und aufeinander reagierender Komponenten. Unsere größte Herausforderung ist es, nach neuen Möglichkeiten innerhalb des Systems zu suchen. So fußt beispielsweise unser Entwurf für die Drenter und Groninger Veenkolonien auf einem strategischen Szenario, bei dem

straitjacket, but to set them up capable of adapting to the users' more and more rapidly changing customs, wishes and needs.

New layers in the ecosystem. We consider public space a subtle ecosystem. It is not a natural but an abstract network of components mutually influencing and reacting to each other. Our greatest challenge is to look for new possibilities within the system.

Thus, for instance, our design for the Veenkolonien suburbs of Drent and Groningen is based on a strategic scenario in which the basic price and subsidies, in interaction with a directed design, form the basis for a new form of landscape development. It is not enough to design the use of public space, it must also be stimulated.

Material selection through experimentation. In order to decide whether certain materials encourage the use of public space in the desired fashion, experimental testing of the "hardware" is important. During the "test phase" especially, a new kind of creativity can develop that sometimes

use

surprise provocative dynamic use of public space

event function intervention new frontiers exploration

Zeit war jahrhundertelang das wichtigste Instrument des Landschaftsarchitekten. Der Raum war nie fertig, es blieb Spielraum für Korrekturen aufgrund veränderter Nutzungen. Die Planer von Karres en Brands schlagen vor, provisorische Räume anzubieten, die sich im Laufe der Zeit unter ihrer Regie weiterentwickeln. Ihre Materialien werden in situ geprüft.

For centuries time was the most important tool used by the landscape architect. A space was never finished; there was room for revisions depending on changing uses. The planners of the Karres en Brands office propose to provide temporary spaces that can continue to develop in the course of time under their direction. Their materials are tested on site.

leads to surprising results. If the commission permits, we aim to separate the development of the design from the planning process. In the Gouvernementsplein square in Bergen op Zoom we began right after the preliminary design was approved with preparations for construction. In a team of planners, the construction company, technical designer and client we voted on the final design and its materials. The result was new ways to use the materials, new techniques of treatment and many on-the-spot experiments and prototypes. How a space develops in the course of time also depends on the lifetime of the materials. Calculating to include the ageing of

Grundpreis und Subventionen im Zusammenspiel mit einem gesteuerten Entwurf die Grundlage für eine neue Form der Landschaftsentwicklung bilden. Es reicht nicht aus, die Nutzung des öffentlichen Raums zu entwerfen, sie muss auch stimuliert werden.

Materialwahl durch Experimente. Um zu entscheiden, ob bestimmte Materialien die Nutzung des öffentlichen Raums auf die gewünschte Weise anregen, ist das experimentelle Erproben der »Hardware« wichtig. Gerade während einer »Testphase« kann sich eine ganz neue Art von Kreativität entfalten, die manchmal zu überraschenden Ergebnissen führt. Wenn es die Auftragslage zulässt, streben wir danach, die Ausarbeitung des Entwurfs aus dem Planungsprozess auszukoppeln.

Beim Platz Gouvernementsplein in Bergen op Zoom begannen wir nach der Annahme des Vorentwurfs gleich mit den Bauvorbereitungen. In einem Team aus Planern, Baufirma, Konstrukteur und Auftraggeber stimmten wir den endgültigen Entwurf und seine Materialien ab. Heraus kamen neue Methoden der Materialverwendung, neue Techniken der Bearbeitung und viele Vor-Ort-Experimente und etliche Prototypen.

Auch von der Lebensdauer der Materialien hängt es ab, wie sich ein Raum im Laufe der Zeit entwickelt. Allzu oft sieht ein Raum nur kurze Zeit so aus, wie die Pläne auf dem Papier es suggeriert haben. Bald aber nutzen sich seine Materialien ab, und der Raum funktioniert nicht mehr wie ursprünglich beabsichtigt. Das Einkalkulieren der Materialalterung hingegen kann einem Entwurf eine zweite Ebene verleihen. Das angestrebte Bild wird in Phasen erreicht, wobei die Zeit ihre Arbeit geräusch- und kostenlos verrichtet. Rost, Moos, Verfärbung und Verfall sind für uns wichtige Entwurfselemente.

Integration des Organisationsprozesses. Nicht nach ästhetischen oder kostentechnischen Kriterien sollten Materialien ausgewählt werden, sondern nach der gewünschten Nutzung. Unser Büro strebt daher an, den Bauprozess mit all seinen bekannten Organisationsstrukturen zum Bestandteil des Entwurfsprozesses werden zu lassen.

Im Projekt Utrecht-Leidsche Rijn (siehe *Topos* 31) haben wir kürzlich mit dem Bau des Parks Hoge Weide begonnen. Der Entwurf wurde ohne Materialangaben und Details angenommen. Er gibt den dreidimensionalen Raumaufbau vor, eine finanzielle Strategie sowie ein Organisationsschema für den Bauablauf, und er beschreibt die zu erwartende Nutzung. Wir entschieden uns dafür, möglichst viele vorhandene Materialien zu verwenden und sie je nach Angebot auszubalancieren mit einem Anteil neuer Materialien. Hardware und Software zusammen sollen ein gut funktionierendes und spannendes Resultat ergeben.

Plädoyer für Planung und Prozess. Die heutige Geschwindigkeit beim Entwerfen und Bauen, insbesondere in den Niederlanden, ist oft ein Problem für die Planer. In einigen Projekten unseres Büros in Hengelo, Venray und Tilburg schlagen wir daher vor, den öffentlichen Raum zunächst teilweise mit provisorischer »Hardware« anzubieten.

Unserer Ansicht nach ermöglichen provisorische Räume eher Austausch, Anpassung oder Erweiterung, wenn die Umgebung es erfordert. Die Materialien werden in situ geprüft. Der »neue öffentliche Raum« ist dann nicht in erster Linie das Endprodukt eines Entwurfsprozesses, sondern kann sich unter Regie verändern. Und damit wird er ein wirklicher Entwurf unserer Zeit, nämlich interaktiv.

the materials can lend the design a second level. The projected image is reached phase by phase, during which time does its job free of noise or costs. Rust, moss, discoloration and decay are important design elements for us.

Integrating the organisation process. Neither aesthetic nor cost criteria but the desired uses should be decisive for the choice of materials. Our office therefore instead to make the building process with all its well-known organisational structures a part of the design process. In the Utrecht-Leidsche Rijn project (see *Topos* 31) we recently began construction on the Hoge Weide Park. The design was approved without information and details on the materials. It provides the three-dimensional spatial structure, a financial strategy and an organisation chart, and it describes the uses to be expected. We hope to use as many materials available on the site as possible and, depending on availability, to balance them with a number of new materials. Hardware and software together are to provide a well functioning and exciting result.

A plea for planning and process. Today's speed in designing and building, especially in The Netherlands, is often a problem for the planners. In some projects by our office in Hengelo, Venray and Tilburg we therefore propose providing public space in part with temporary "hardware" for the time being. In our opinion, provisional spaces allow more communication, adaptation or expansion when this is called for by the surroundings. The materials are tested *in situ*. Then the "new public space" is not primarily the final product of a design process but can change under supervision. And thus it becomes a true design of our time: namely, interactive.

Wenig, das aber richtig

A little means a lot

In einer Welt, die immer bequemer, flexibler und schneller wird, aber dennoch abstrakt und unüberschaubar bleibt, kommt der Landschaftsarchitektur eine Vermittlerrolle zu. Wer sich an den schieren Möglichkeiten des Marktes orientiert, lässt sich schnell von den bunten, explodierenden Bildern verführen, von der Cut-and-Paste-Mentalität, vom überbordenden Mix der Materialien. Um Orte zu definieren, Authentizität zu vermitteln und vielleicht sogar eine »Gegenwelt« zu schaffen, müssen Landschaftsarchitekten auswählen – weniges, das aber richtig. Dabei gelten die alten Regeln: Bäume wachsen immer noch nicht in den Himmel (selbst wenn Computerspiele es suggerieren), und gute Landschaftsarchitektur ist auf Zeit gegründet (selbst wenn die Instant-Landschaften mancher Flower-Shows das Gegenteil vorgaukeln). Beim Auswählen der Materialien für den Freiraum bleibt es daher wichtig, den Kontext nicht zu ignorieren, Orientierung zu bieten, die Konstruktion nicht zu verhehlen und Altern in Würde zu ermöglichen.

Philipp Sattler

Holz für das Jugendfreizeitzentrum Buchholz. In der neuen Berliner Vorstadt Berlin-Buchholz dient das Haus mit seinem Garten als Begegnungsstätte für Jugendliche. Schollenartige Bauteile fügen sich zu einem polygonalen Baukörper, dessen Dynamik wir im Freiraum aufgenommen haben. Neben einer Rasenfläche gibt es Räume für das Tischtennis- und Basketballspiel und zum Fahrrad-Reparieren. Bestimmendes Material ist Kiefernholz, zum einen als Zaun und Umfassung der Mülltonnen, zum anderen als Sitzelement zwischen Plattenfläche und Rasen. Das Material nimmt Bezug zur teilweise sichtbaren Unterkonstruktion der Eternitfassade, die den Ort farblich dominiert. Die Bänke bieten genügend Ecken zum Sitzen, Rauchen und Quatschen in Cliquen, Zweiergruppen oder

In a world that is getting more comfortable, more flexible and faster all the time while remaining abstract and unpredictable nonetheless, it befits landscape architecture to play the role of mediator. Anyone oriented on market possibilities alone will soon be seduced by the colourful exploding images, the cut-and-paste mentality, and the riotous mix of materials. But to define a place, to communicate authenticity, and perhaps even to create a contrasting world, landscape architects must be selective: use little but use it right. The old rules apply: trees still cannot grow

Schmale Budgets, komplexe Ansprüche und maximale Verfügbarkeit bestimmen heute die Materialwahl. Da tun klare Konzepte not.

Small budgets, complex demands and maximum accessibility determine the choice of materials today. That calls for clear concepts.

Den bunten, explodierenden Bildern etwas entgegenzusetzen, lautet heute die Aufgabe der Landschaftsarchitekten. Schlichte, sorgfältig ausgewählte Materialien schaffen klare Räume.

Countering the colourful exploding images that result from a cut-and-paste approach is the task facing landscape architects today. Plain, carefully selected materials create clear spaces.

sky-high (despite computer games that may suggest otherwise) and good landscape architecture is still based on time (even though the instant landscapes of some flower shows lead us to believe the opposite). In choosing materials for open spaces it is therefore still important not to ignore the context, to provide orientation, not to conceal the construction, and to allow the completed project to age with dignity.

Wood for the Buchholz Youth Centre. In the new suburb of Berlin-Buchholz, this house and its garden serve as a place for young people to get together. The slabs forming the building join into a polygonal structure whose dynamics we picked up in the open space design. Besides a lawn there are areas for playing table tennis and basketball and for repairing bicycles. The prevailing material is pinewood, used on the one hand as a fence and around the dust-bins, and on the other as a seating element between the paved areas and the lawn. This material refers to the wooden framework partly visible under the asbestos cement facade that dominates the site in terms of colour.

The benches provide plenty of corners and bends to sit, smoke and gossip in groups, in pairs or alone. Together, they combine to form a unified whole. Their construction is both robust and simple. They are made of beams glued together into one massive block, as unadorned as suburban reality, and ready to be scribbled on and carved into. The surface of the wood offers itself to the users: they are to appropriate it and leave behind traces of their presence.

Concrete for the residential courts of the Goertzallee extension. This residential site on the southern periphery of Berlin consists of a narrow lot

allein. Insgesamt fügen sie sich dennoch zu einer Gesamtform. Die Konstruktion, so robust wie einfach, besteht aus Leimbindern, die zum massiven Block gefasst wurden: ungeschönt wie die Realität im Vorort, und bereit, bekritzelt und zerschnitzt zu werden. Die Oberfläche des Holzes bietet sich den Benutzern an – sie sollen sie sich aneignen und darauf ihre Spuren hinterlassen.

Beton für die Wohnhöfe der verlängerten Goertzallee. Die Wohnanlage am Südrand Berlins steht auf einem schmalen Grundstück, die Wohnhäuser sind schräg-senkrecht zur Grundstückslänge positioniert und geben Zwischenräume frei. Die Freiräume sollen die Reihung ergänzen. Die »Höfe« zwischen den Gebäuden unterscheiden sich nur durch Feinheiten wie die

Kiefernholz prägt den Garten des Berliner Jugendfreizeitheims. Als Sitzelement trennt es den Rasen von der Pflasterfläche und bietet Ecken fürs Zusammensitzen. Die robuste Konstruktion besteht aus Leimbindern, die zu massiven Blöcken gefasst wurden.

Pine predominates in the garden of the youth centre in Berlin. In the seating element it separates the lawn from the paved area and provides corners for gossiping in groups, or in pairs. The robust structure consists of beams glued together to form massive blocks.

with a row of buildings set diagonally and at right angles to the direction of the lot, leaving spaces free in between. The open space concept aimed at filling in the row.

Courtyards were formed between the individual buildings. They differ only in details such as plantings. What they have in common is an axial geometric spatial structure, created by two different types of concrete elements. One is a large slice of wall shielding the court towards the north from access on foot or by car. The other is a strip

Bepflanzung. Gemeinsam ist ihnen eine axial-geometrische Raumstruktur, geschaffen durch zwei verschiedene Typen von Betonelementen. Zum einen schirmt jeweils eine große Mauer-scheibe den Hof nach Norden von Zugang und Zufahrt ab. Zum anderen setzt ein Mauer-Band die Parallele zum jeweiligen Baukörper in den Raum. Der Weißbeton kontrastiert bewusst mit den bunten Putzfassaden. Die Mauern spannen den Außenbereich auf und markieren ihn als Raum. Ihre schlichte Geometrie bildet das Gerüst, auf der die Ausstattungselemente und Beläge jeden Gartenhof auf seine Weise materialisieren. An der Mauer-scheibe lassen sich die Qualitäten des Betons erkennen. Auf der Nordseite schlicht gehalten, aber subtil profiliert, schirmt die Mauer den Hof aku-stisch und visuell zur Einfahrt ab. Auf seiner Südseite nimmt sie eine Sitz-bank auf und reflektiert das Sonnenlicht, wird zum Fokus des Hofes. Der exakten Form des Betons steht der Wandel seiner Oberfläche durch die Witterung gegenüber – sie wird seine haptischen Qualitäten mit der Zeit sicher noch erhöhen.

Stahl für das Werksgelände der Trumpf Sachsen GmbH. Als dieses mittel-ständische Unternehmen in der Sächsischen Schweiz seine Produktionsge-bäude erweiterte, bekam unser Büro den Auftrag, die Außenanlagen neu zu

Im Freiraum setzt sich die Dy-namik des polygonalen Bau-körpers mit schollenartigen Flächen fort. Das Material ihrer Umfassungen leitet sich ab von der hölzernen Unter-konstruktion der Fassade, die zum Teil unter den halbtrans-parenten Eternitplatten zu erkennen ist.

The dynamics of the polygonal building are carried forth in the layered surfaces of the open space. The material used for the borders around them refers to the wooden frame-work of the facade partly visi-ble under the semitransparent asbestos cement panels.

Grounds of the Buchholz-West Youth Centre, Berlin, Germany
Client: ERGERO
Landscape architects: Kiefer, Berlin (Susanne Quednau, project head)
Architects: Barkow Leibinger, Berlin
Area: 1,200 square metres
Planning: 1993 – 1994
Construction: 1995 – 1996
Costs: DEM 224,000

of wall tracing a line parallel to the adjacent building in the courtyard space. The white concrete we used contrasts intentionally with the coloured stucco of the facades.

The walls open up the outdoor area and mark it as a space. Their plain geometry provides a framework on which the outdoor furniture and ground covers cause each courtyard to materialise in its own way. The slice of wall reveals the properties of concrete. Kept plain but subtly profiled on the north side, the wall shields the court acoustically and visually from the entrance. On the south side it incorporates a bench and reflects the sunlight, becoming the focal point of the court. The precise shape of the concrete contrasts with the changes brought about on its surface by the climate. Its textures will probably become more pronounced with time.

Steel for the Trumpf Sachsen GmbH factory. When this medium-sized firm in the mountainous region called Sächsische Schweiz (Saxon Switzerland) expanded its production plant, we were commissioned to create a new concept for the grounds. The key element of the design is the so-called landscape lane, a man-made landscape within the open landscape. This lane provides outdoor space for the employees as well as for transport vehicles driving from one part of the factory grounds to another.

The requirements of the enterprise demanded that the area be divided up into strips. This hence became a meaningful design principle. The firm's range of products led us to use metal as a theme in the open space. Water-polished steel strips in the stepway were custom-made to correspond to individually developed details. They pick up the material of the new building's facades. The clear

konzipieren. Schlüsselelement des Entwurfes ist die sogenannte Landschaftsschneise, eine gebaute Landschaft innerhalb der »freien« Landschaft. Die Schneise bietet Freiraum für die Mitarbeiter, aber auch für die Trans-

Zwei Betonelemente bestimmen die Wohnhöfe der Berliner Goertzallee: eine Mauerscheibe als Schirm zur Einfahrt und ein Mauerband als strukturiende Linie parallel zu den Wohnbauten. Die Höfe unterscheiden sich nur durch Details der Vegetation und der Beläge voneinander.

Two concrete elements characterise the residential courts in Goertzallee in Berlin: a slice of wall shielding the court from access and a strip of wall forming a structuring line parallel to the buildings. The yards differ from each other only in details of vegetation and paving.

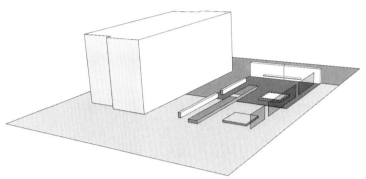

portfahrzeuge, die von einem Teil des Fabrik-geländes zum anderen fahren. Betriebliche Ansprüche verlangten nach einer Gliederung in Streifen – sie war deshalb als Entwurfsprinzip sinnvoll. Die Produktpalette des Unternehmens reizte dazu, auch im Freiraum Metall zum Thema zu erheben. Wasserpolierter Edelstahl, nach individuell entwickelten Details gefertigt, nimmt in der Treppenanlage das Material der Neubau-Fassaden auf. Die klare Form und kühle Ausstrahlung des Materials kontrastiert mit dem Basaltschotter und -pflaster der Wege wie auch mit dem blauem Lavendel und den weißen Strauchrosen der Beete. An einem Produktionsstandort geht es weniger um Atmosphäre als um praktische Aspekte. Stahl leistet hier gute Dienste: In Gestalt von Kantenbändern, Treppenwangen und Handläufen spannt er die Fäden eines Netzes, in welches Beläge und Ausstattungselemente »eingehängt« werden. Der Reiz liegt im Spiel mit Serialität und Anordnung, in der Perfektion der Details und in der Komposition von Alltagsma-

Die Betonmauer im Norden eines jeden Wohnhofes gibt sich zur Einfahrt hin als kühler, aber subtil profilierter Blick- und Lärmschild. Zum Hof hin speichert und reflektiert ihre Südseite die Sonne und lädt zum Verweilen auf der vorgehängten Bank.

The concrete wall along the north of each courtyard presents a cool but subtly profiled shield from view and noise towards the entrance. Its south side facing the yard stores and reflects the sunshine and invites residents to linger on the attached bench.

forms and the cool feeling of this material contrast with the basalt crushed stone and paving along the pathways as well as with the blue laven-

terial zu einem Gesamtbild, das im Sinne industrieller Produktion attraktiv ist, nämlich reduziert, ergonomisch und schön anzusehen. Wie die drei Beispiele zeigen, hat jedes Freiraumprojekt seine Atmosphäre, setzt eigene Ak-

Residential courts of the Goertzallee extension, Berlin-Zehlendorf, Germany
Client: GEHAG Berlin
Landscape architects: Kiefer, Berlin
Architects: GEHAG construction department, Berlin (project),
Sadowski & Lebioda, Berlin (detailled plans and project management)
Area: 9,700 square metres
Planning: 1994 – 1995
Construction: 1996 – 1997
Costs: DEM 1,560,000

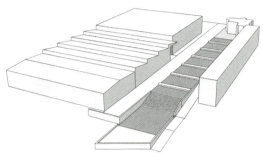

der and white rosebushes in the flowerbeds. For a manufacturing site, practicability is more of a priority in the grounds than atmosphere. Steel is very serviceable in this case. In the form of bands along the risers and of strings and handrails on the tep, it creates a frame in which to "hang" the paving and furnishing elements.

Its charm lies in the play with serial qualities and placement, in the perfection of details, and in arranging everyday materials into an overall picture that is attractive in the sense of industrial production, namely, simplified, ergonomic and beautiful to look at.

As these examples show, each project has an atmosphere of its own, with its own focus. What the designs have in common is that each place is given an order, the individual elements in it serve as a backbone, and the material used provides a leitmotiv. The use of a certain material today involves coming to terms with conditions in post-industrial society: small budgets, complex demands and maximum accessibility.

Ready-mades and (new) materials should be used such that the polish won't rub off right away, in every sense of the word. Flashy technical effects are seldom of any use. Landscaped grounds, like gardens, must last.

Eine »gebaute« Landschafts-schneise gliedert ein Werksge-lände in der »freien« Land-schaft der Sächsischen Schweiz. Es kam den Betriebsabläufen entgegen, den Freiraum in Streifen anzuordnen. Basalt-schotter und -pflaster kontra-stiert mit blauem Lavendel und weißen Strauchrosen.

A man-made landscape strip subdivides the factory grounds of a tool production plant in the open landscape of the so-called Switzerland of Saxony. The operations call for the grounds to be divided up into strips. Basalt crushed stone and paving contrast with blue lavender and white rosebushes.

zente. Gemeinsam ist den Entwürfen, dass jeder Ort eine Ordnung erhält und einzelne Elemente die Funktion eines gebauten Rückgrats überneh- men, mit ihrem Material als Leitmotiv. Materialverwendung heißt heute, sich mit den Bedingungen der post-industriellen Gesellschaft auseinander- zusetzen: schmale Budgets, komplexe Ansprüche und maximale Verfügbar- keit. Es sollte darauf ankommen, mit Ready-mades und (neuen) Materiali- en so umzugehen, dass der Lack im wahrsten Sinne des Wortes nicht sofort ab ist. Schnelle technische Effekte helfen selten weiter. Außenanlagen wie Gärten müssen dauern.

Metall auch im Freiraum zu verwenden, bot sich bei einem metallverarbeitenden Betrieb an. Wasserpolierter Edelstahl spannt in der Form von Kan- tenbändern, Treppenwangen und Handläufen ein feines metallisches Netz auf, das mit anderen Materialien ausgefüllt wurde.

Using metal in the open space seemed appropriate for a met- al tool production plant. Wa- ter-polished high-grade steel weaves a fine metallic net, in the form of bands along the risers, of strings and of rail- ings on the steps, which was filled in with other materials.

Grounds of the Trumpf Sachsen GmbH, Neukirch, Lausitz, Germany
Client: Trumpf Sachsen GmbH, Neukirch
Landscape architects: Kiefer, Berlin (Tancredi Capatti, project head)
Architecture: Barkow Leibinger, Berlin
Area: 16,000 square metres
Planning: 1999 – 2000
Construction: 2000
Costs: DEM 1,300,000

Public Design: das Vertraute modulieren

Public design: Modulating the familiar

Maria Auböck
János Kárász

Mobiliar für den öffentlichen Raum muss pflegeleicht und robust sein und soll auch eine poetische ästhetische Aussage transportieren.

Furnishings for public spaces must be low-maintenance and robust while making a poetic aesthetic statement at the same time.

Erst durch Idee und Entwurf werden die Materialien des Freiraums zu einem größeren Ganzen. Neue und weiterentwickelte Werkstoffe, wie etwa Asphalt im 19. oder Glas im 20. Jahrhundert, haben unsere öffentlichen Räume nachhaltig verändert. Und sie verändern sich weiter: einerseits durch immer neue Anforderungen und die schier unbegrenzten Möglichkeiten ihrer Nutzung, andererseits durch die »Konkurrenz« eines neuen öffentlichen Raumes, nämlich dem der elektronischen Medien. So paradox es klingt, der Gebrauchsdruck auf den öffentlichen Raum nimmt ständig zu und verschwindet zugleich im Virtuellen. Mit den Mitteln der Landschaftsarchitektur arbeiten wir an der materiellen Vielfalt der Wirklichkeit. Dabei bedeutet Vielfalt nicht die Anwesenheit zahlreicher Materialien in ein und demselben Projekt. Vielmehr wollen wir uns nicht von vornherein beschränken, sondern offen bleiben und aus einem reichen Reservoir an Materialien für einen bestimmten Ort die richtigen auswählen. Schließlich müssen sie der Spannung standhalten zwischen Mehrfachnutzung, Raumschichtung und Bedeutung. Zu den vielfältigen Bestandteilen

It takes ideas and design to make materials for open spaces add up to a larger whole. New and further-developed building materials, such as asphalt in the 19th century and glass in the 20th, have changed our public spaces forever. And they are continuing to change: on the one hand to meet continuously new demands and their sheer unlimited potential for use, on the other through "competition" from a new kind of public space, namely that of the electronic media. As paradox as it may sound, the pressure of heavy use on public space is growing steadily but disappearing at the same time into virtual space.

Using the means available to landscape architecture, we are working on the material diversity of reality. This diversity does not mean the presence of a lot of different materials in one and the same project. Rather, without limiting ourselves from the outset, we intend to be open and to select from an abundant store of materials those that are right for a certain place. After all, we must maintain the tension between multiple use, layered spaces and inherent meaning. Among the various materials for open spaces we of course include the smell of coffee and the crunch of gravel, the play of light and shade on a concrete bench, the changing colours on the stone tiles of a square after the rain, the consistency of water in a park between fog and ice... everything that virtual space does not provide.

Furniture, too, is a part of public space. It must stand up to the most challenging conditions: it must be low-maintenance and vandalism-proof and, nevertheless, always make an aesthetic statement.

The shape of a bench, retaining wall or gangway not only obeys functional considerations but

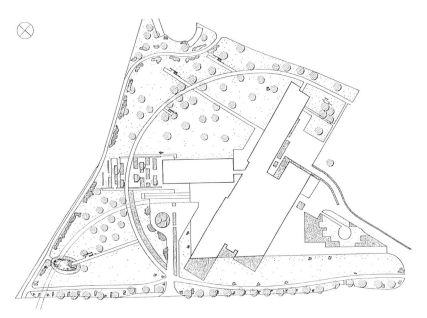

is also a vehicle for meaning. It calls forth expectations and serves as a screen for projecting wishes, desires, and even fears. Furniture must therefore be chosen carefully. Instead of stuffing open spaces arbitrarily with fashionable items found in catalogues, we insist on planning and design innovation in public design.

Materials in open spaces, and especially the furniture, evoke astonishment, satisfaction, curiosity, the urge to go exploring, or a feeling of security, depending on whether the planners used building materials and objects that are familiar or unusual.

The choice between the one or the other expresses the conditions involved in the production and use of each. Last but not least, it also says something about the willingness to take a chance, the non-conformity or the playfulness that the client and planner are committed to.

When we design a space with common materials and furniture we always ask ourselves: to what extent can the familiar be modulated, can surprise be deferred to the second glance, and can new elements be introduced with a minimum of irritation into familiar ones? Finally, we also have to take into consideration how an object is going to age in public space, what patina it will acquire with time. It must be technically and aesthetically enduring.

Hartberg provincial hospital. The quiet section of the park consists of a niche-like expansion of a branch of the pathway. It is paved with setts made of Stainz gneiss, a regional stone and therefore a familiar material.

Staggered, wedge-shaped and squared concrete blocks with (removable) wooden covers projecting from the slope provide seating in the

des Freiraums zählen wir durchaus auch den Kaffeegeruch und das Knirschen des Kieses, das Spiel von Licht und Schatten auf einer Betonbank, die changierenden Farben auf den Steinplatten eines Stadtplatzes nach dem Regen, die Konsistenz des Wassers im Park zwischen Nebel und Eis... all das, was der virtuelle Raum nicht bietet. Auch Möbel sind Teil des öffentlichen Raumes. Unter schwierigsten Bedingungen müssen sie sich bewähren: Pflegeleicht und vandalensicher müssen sie sein und dabei stets auch eine ästhe-

Im Hartberger Krankenhaus bietet der sorgsam gestaltete Ruheplatz, gepflastert mit regionalem Gneis und Sitzmöbeln aus Beton und kanadischer Zeder, Patienten wie Stadtbewohnern Raum zum Ausruhen.

At the Hartberg hospital a thoughtfully designed quiet corner of the park, paved with local gneiss and equipped with furniture in concrete and Canadian cedar, provides room for both patients and town residents to recover.

tische Aussage transportieren. Die Form einer Bank, einer Stützmauer oder eines Steges folgt nicht bloß funktionalen Aspekten, sondern trägt auch Bedeutung, schürt Erwartungen und dient als Projektionsfläche für Wünsche, Sehnsüchte, mitunter auch Ängste. Mobiliar will deshalb sorgsam ausge-

Park of Hartberg provincial hospital, Steiermark, Austria
Client: KAGes, Steiermärkische Krankenanstalten GmbH (provincial hospitals)
Landscape architects: Auböck & Kárász, Vienna
Architecture: Klaus Kada, Vienna
Area: 3 hectares
Planning: 1997 – 1999
Realisation: 1999
Costs: DEM 900,000.

sucht sein. Statt die Freiräume wahllos mit modischer Katalogware vollzustopfen, fordern wir planerische und gestalterische Innovation im Public Design.

Die Materialien des Freiraums, und insbesondere seine Möbel, rufen Staunen, Zufriedenheit, Neugierde, Entdeckerlust oder Sicherheitsempfinden hervor, je nachdem, ob die Planer vertraute Werkstoffe und Objekte einsetzen, oder außergewöhnliche. Die Entscheidung für das eine oder andere drückt die jeweiligen Bedingungen der Produktion und des Gebrauchs aus, und nicht zuletzt auch die Risikobereitschaft, den Widerspruchsgeist oder auch das lustvolle Spiel, dem sich Bauherr und Planer verschreiben.

Wenn wir versuchen, den Raum mit selbstverständlichen Materialien und Möbeln zu gestalten, dann fragen wir uns immer: Wie weit lässt sich das Vertraute modulieren, die Überraschung für den zweiten Blick aufhe-

garden. The place is inviting for both patients and local urban residents, a both public and (almost) private place. Seats and tabletops made of Canadian cedar provide an exotic touch.

Blumau spa park. The park's furniture thrives on its jarring effects on familiar elements. The

Die für den Thermenpark Blumau entworfenen Parkmöbel zaubern eine poetische Stimmung hervor, ergänzt von mediterranen Trockenmauern aus Gneis. Die Brücke aus Lärchenholz lädt mit ihrem breiten Geländer zum Anlehnen und Schauen ein.

The furniture designed for the park of the Blumau spa evokes a poetic atmosphere. The Mediterranean dry walls made of gneiss provide the finishing touch. The larch bridge has wide railings that invite people to lean on them and enjoy the view.

ben, das Neue als minimale Irritation des Herkömmlichen einsetzen? Schließlich müssen wir auch das Altern eines Objekts im öffentlichen Raum mitbedenken, und die Patina, die es mit der Zeit erhalten wird. Es muss technisch und ästhetisch haltbar sein.

bridge across the Safen Brook, looking light and Japanese from afar, turns out to be very solid when you come to cross it. The railing is shaped into a slab you can lean on. The untreated larch

Blumau spa park, Steiermark, Austria
Client: province of Steiermark and municipality of Blumau
Landscape architects: Auböck & Kárász, Vienna
Area: central section 7.5 hectares
Planning: 1997 – 1999
Construction: 2000 – 2003
Costs: DEM 1.5 million

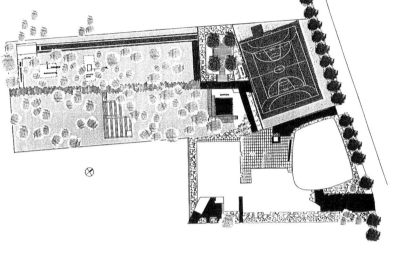

will soon acquire a silvery patina. The deck chairs in the park are clearly lower than traditional park furniture, providing unusual views and creating the impression of a private space. The back-to-back benches allow you sit in various positions: on one side you perch as stiffly as in a church pew, on the other you relax and enjoy a wide-ranging view of the landscape.

Some of the freestanding dry walls made of local gneiss are suitable for sitting or reclining on. In combination with the perennials, they create a Mediterranean atmosphere and are effective because of their poetic alienation of apparently normal features.

Garden of a school on Gerichtsgasse, Vienna. The central feature is an educational nature pond. On two sides it is framed by a raised larch

pier. On the other two the water spills naturally onto a gravel bed. The informal contours contrast with the architectural clarity of the wooden planking.

Garden of a school in Gerichtsgasse, Vienna, Austria
Client: City of Vienna
Landscape architects: Auböck & Kárász, Vienna
Architects: Sepp Müller + eichinger oder knechtl
Area: 0.6 hectares
Planning: 1998 – 1999
Realisation: 1999
Costs: DEM 200,000.

Landeskrankenhaus Hartberg. Der Ruheplatz im Park entsteht aus der nischenhaften Erweiterung eines Stichweges. Er ist mit Stainzerplatten gepflastert, einem regionalen Gneis und deshalb einem vertrauten Material. Gegeneinander versetzte, keilförmig aus dem Hang ragende Betonquader mit (abnehmbaren) Holzauflagen fügen sich zu Sitzen im Garten – ein Ort, der sowohl Patienten wie Stadtbewohner einlädt, ein öffentlicher und zugleich beinahe privater Platz, dessen Sitze und Tischplatte aus kanadischer Zeder einen Hauch von Exotik vermitteln.

Thermenpark Blumau. Die Möblierung des Parks lebt von vielfältigen Irritationen des Vertrauten: Die von weitem japanisch-leicht anmutende Brücke über den Safenbach entpuppt sich beim Hinüberschreiten als äußerst stabil, das Geländer ist als Tafel zum Anlehnen ausgebildet; das unbehandelte Lärchenholz erhält schnell eine silbrige Patina. Die Liegen des Parks sind deutlich niedriger als traditionelle Parkmöbel, bieten ungewohnte Ausblicke und vermitteln das Gefühl eines privaten Raumes. Die Doppelbänke ermöglichen Sitzen in unterschiedlichen Haltungen: auf der einen Seite steif wie auf einer Kirchenbank, auf der anderen entspannt und mit weitem Blick über die Landschaft. Manche der freistehenden Trockenmauern aus örtlichem Gneis eignen sich zum Sitzen oder Liegen. Sie erzeugen mit den Stauden eine mediterrane Atmosphäre und wirken durch die poetische Verfremdung des vermeintlich Selbstverständlichen.

Schulgarten in der Wiener Gerichtsgasse. Zentrales Element ist der Lehrteich. Seine Wasserfläche wird auf zwei Seiten von einem aufgeständerten Lärchen-Steg gefasst. Auf den anderen zwei Seiten schwappt das Wasser frei auf ein Kiesbett. Die freie Kontur kontrastiert mit der architektonischen Klarheit der Holzroste.

Früher eine Brauerei, heute eine Schule mit Flächen mit Sport und Spiel. Herzstück des Schulgartens ist der Lehrteich mit einem aufgeständerten Steg aus Lärchenholz.

Formerly a brewery, now a school with grounds for sports and games. The heart of the school garden is an educational nature pond with a raised larch pier.

Authors

Thorbjörn Andersson, who was born in 1954, is a landscape architect with diplomas gained in Sweden and the USA. He works with the FFNS office in Stockholm and has designed a number of urban landscapes in Sweden as well as in Portugal and Germany. Some of them have won awards in Sweden and abroad. He has written numerous articles and books about landscape architecture. In spring 2001 he will teach at Harvard University in the USA.

Maria Auböck studied architecture in Vienna and landscape architecture at the Technical University in Munich-Weihenstephan. She has taught in the USA and been a professor at the Munich Academy of Art since 1999. In 1985 she established her own office in Vienna, joined by János Kárász in 1987.

Henri Bava was born in 1957. He studied biology at Paris-Orsay University and gained his diploma in landscape architecture at the Ecole Nationale Supérieure du Paysage in Versailles (ENSP) in 1984. He founded the Agence Ter office with Michel Hoessler and Olivier Philippe in Paris in 1985. From 1987 to 1997 he taught at ENSP. Since 1998 he has been a professor at the Institute for Landscape and Garden at Karlsruhe University. Agence Ter established a branch office in Karlsruhe in 2000.

Alfred Berger, who was born in 1961, studied architecture at the Technical University in Vienna and the Vienna Academy of Fine Arts with Professor Timo Pentilää. From 1992 to 1994 he worked in a partnership with Pentilää and Werner Krismer. From 1994 to 1997 he was Assistant Professor at the Academy. He has worked in office partnerships and collaborated on projects with Tiina Parkkinen. They founded Berger + Parkkinen Architects in 1995.

Jonas Berglund is a landscape architect. He founded the Niveau office in Stockholm with Åsa Drougge and Göran Lindberg.

Stefano Boeri, who was born in 1956, is an architect. He teaches urban design at the University of Genoa and the Polytechnic in Milan. He is currently lecturing at the Postgraduate Laboratory of Architecture of the Berlage Institute in Amsterdam. Since 1998 he has been the managing curator of the architecture section of the Milan Triennale. He writes regularly for the cultural supplement of the financial daily, *Il Sole 24 Ore.*

Bart Brands, who was born in 1962, studied at the Horticultural College in Boskoop and at the Department of Urban Development at the Academy of Architecture in Rotterdam and Amsterdam. He worked for the municipalities of Diemen and The Hague, and went on to join the B+B office in Amsterdam in 1989. Since 1997 he has run his own practice, Karres en Brands, together with Sylvia Karres.

Lorenz Dexler, who was born in 1968, studied landscape architecture at the Technical University of Hannover. He has been collaborating with Martin Rein-Cano since 1997.

Adriaan Geuze, who was born in 1960, studied landscape architecture at the Agricultural University of Wageningen and gained his diploma in 1987. He founded West 8 landscape architects in Rotterdam in 1987. He has submitted various competition entries and won the Rotterdam Maaskant Prize for Young Architects in 1995.

Johanna Gibbons graduated from Heriot Watt University in 1983 and worked in the USA and South Africa as project landscape architect on urban renewal projects. She established J & L Gibbons in London in 1986 with partner and husband Luke Gibbons. Her book, Urban streetscapes: A workbook for designers, was published in 1991.

Shauna Gillies-Smith gained her Bachelor of Arts at Queen's University in Kingston, Canada, her Bachelor of Architecture at the University of British Columbia in Vancouver, and her Master of Urban Design at Harvard Graduate School of Design. She has been principal and senior designer at Martha Schwartz, Inc. in Cambridge, USA, from February to July 1996 and since June 1997.

Bengt Isling was born in 1954. He studied landscape architecture at the Swedish College of Agriculture, Ultuna, and in Alnarp. He began working as a landscape architect in 1979 and went on to join the Nyréns architecture office in 1987. He teaches at Ultuna.

János Kárász studied architecture and sociology in Vienna. His professional fields are architecture and open space and landscape design. He has also produced several sociological and cultural studies, film projects, museum and exhibition concepts as well as exhibition designs. He teaches in Vienna and Budapest. He has been working in a partnership with Maria Auböck since 1987.

Martin Knuijt was born in 1966. He graduated in landscape architecture from the Agricultural University of Wageningen in 1991. He worked on various interdisciplinary teams before joining the Okra landscape architects office. His projects to date include the design for the open space masterplan of the inner-city plan for Amsterdam as well as use and mobility studies. He has published widely on urban planning.

Matthias Krebs was born 1965. He lives and works as a landscape architect in Winterthur, Switzerland. After training as a gardener specialised in perennials, he studied landscape architecture at the Technical College in Rapperswil. He is a member of the Association of Swiss Landscape Architects and partner in the office of Rotzler Krebs Partner Landscape Architects, with offices in Winterthur and Gockhausen.

Bernd Krüger, who was born in 1949, studied garden design and landscape architecture in Erfurt and has worked in various architecture and landscape planning offices. He started working as a freelance landscape architect in 1980, concentrating on recreation areas and private open space. He established a practice in Stuttgart with Hubert Möhrle in 1986 and has taught at Nürtingen Polytechnic. A branch office of Krüger + Möhrle

landscape architects was opened in Berlin in 1991.

Bernard Lassus studied at Ecole Nationale Supérieure des Beaux-Arts and Atelier Fernand Léger. Since 1991 he has been the director of the graduate program on "Gardens, Landscape, Territory" at the Ecole d'Architecture de Paris-La Villette and at the Ecole des Hautes Etudes en Sciences Sociales. He has been a professor at the University of Pennsylvania since 1995. He has taken part in numerous competitions and has been a consultant for many projects. His numerous publications, exhibitions and awards were honoured by the Grand Prix National du Paysage in 1996.

Karel Loeff, who was born in 1969, studied art history at the University of Utrecht between 1987 and 1994. Specialising in architectural history, he wrote a thesis on the design and construction of the 19th-century castle village of Haarzuilens. From 1994 to 1999 he was responsible for the selection of listed state monuments (1850 – 1940) in the province of Utrecht, preparing cultural

and architectural historical studies for municipalities and private companies. He also presented a television documentary on industrial heritage and water management.

Stefan Leppert was born in 1959. After training in banking and horticulture, he studied landscape architecture at Osnabrück Polytechnic. He has worked in practices in Osnabrück and Hamburg, was on the editorial team of *Garten + Landschaft* from 1995 – 2000, and established as a free-lance journalist since then.

Tiina Parkkinen, who was born in Vienna in 1965, studied architecture at the Vienna Academy of Fine Arts under Professor Timo Penttilä. She founded Berger + Parkkinen Architects with Alfred Berger in 1995.

Carme Pinòs was born in 1954. She graduated from the School of Architecture in Barcelona in 1979. She founded an office with Enric Miralles in Barcelona, where she worked from 1983 to 1991. In 1991 she set up her own practice, combining teaching, lec-

turing and participating in several international competitions. She was awarded the Spanish national architecture prize for the Boarding School in Morella in 1995.

Martin Rein-Cano was born in Buenos Aires in 1967. After studying art history in Frankfurt am Main and landscape architecture at the Technical University of Hannover, he worked for the Kiefer office in Berlin from 1994 to 1996. He founded his own office, Topotek 1, in Berlin in 1996.

Christ-Jan van Rooij was born in 1963. He studied landscape architecture at the Agricultural University of Wageningen. Starting in 1990, he worked for the city of Apeldoorn and for the Stichts Cultureel Erfgoed foundation in Utrecht. He founded the Okra landscape architects office with three landscape architect partners in 1994. He concentrates on design management and the realisation of large-scale urban planning projects.

Stefan Rotzler, who was born in 1953, lives in Zurich. He is a member of

the Association of Swiss Landscape Architects and has been working as a freelance landscape architect since 1980, mainly in open space and town planning. He is a partner with Rotzler Krebs Partner Landscape Architects, with offices in Winterthur and Gockhausen.

Philipp Sattler was born in Munich in 1966. After training and work in horticulture and landscape contracting, he studied landscape planning at Berlin Technical University and at Ecole Nationale Supérieure du Paysage in Versailles, and later worked for various journals. He lives in Berlin and works for the landscape architect Gabriele Kiefer.

Martha Schwartz is a landscape architect and artist. She gained a Bachelor of Fine Arts degree from the University of Michigan in 1973, studied landscape architecture at Harvard University's Graduate School of Design from 1976 to 1977, and graduated from the University of Michigan with a Master of Landscape Architecture degree in 1977. She is the lead designer on each project undertaken by her office, and she has received numerous American Society of Landscape Architects national design awards for her projects. She is a professor at the Harvard Graduate School of Design, where she teaches an advanced landscape architecture design studio. Her work has been widely published.

Giordano Tironi, who was born in 1956, studied architecture in Geneva. He has been working in the fields of architecture, public space and landscape since 1982. He teaches at the University of Geneva and the School of Architecture in Grenoble. He was the editor-in-chief of the journal *Rassegna* in Milan and has had numerous books and articles published.

Nicole Uhrig was born in 1970. She studied biology at Kaiserslautern University and landscape planning at the Technical University of Berlin and Escola Técnica Superior d'Arquitectura in Barcelona, specialising in landscape architecture and urban planning. She works for ST raum a landscape architects.

Walter Vetsch, born 1951 in Zurich, Switzerland. 1972-75 Study of landscape architecture at Rapperswil Intercantonal Technical College. 1976-78 Employment at the Hunizker landscape architecture practice, Basel. 1979-83 Employment at the Stöckli + Kienast practice, Wettingen. 1984-95 Proprietor of Walter Vetsch Landscape Architects, Zurich. 1996 Cofoundation of Vetsch, Nipkow Partners, Zurich.

Translations

German/English:
Almuth Seebohm: 4, 6, 49, 65, 80, 84, 89, 96, 100-108; Judith Harrison: 18, 30, 40, 62;Bruce Roberts: 22, 27, 54, 57, 72
Dutch/German:
Beate Rupprecht: 72, 84
English/German:
Lisa Diedrich: 12, 15; Ursula Poblotzki: 37, 45, 80; Cora Lorke: 33, 76
French/German:
Lisa Diedrich: 22, 54, 62
Spanish/German:
Lisa Diedrich: 30

Photo credits

Helge Tschern/Monster Verlag: 7
Nicole Uhrig: 8, 9 (2)
Büro Kiefer: 10
Jeroen Musch: 12, 14 (2)
Studio Boeri: 15
Francesco Jodice: 16, 17 (2)
Ruedi Walti: 19 (2), 20, 21
Giordano Tironi: 22, 23 (4), 24 (2), 25 (2)
Hanns Joosten: 28 (3), 29 (2)
Duccio Malagamba: 32 (2)
Åke Lindman: 34, 35 (2), 36, 82
Olof Thiel: 37, 38 (4), 39
Berger + Parkkinen: 40
Christian Richters: 43 top
Jiri Havran: 43 bottom
Alan Ward: 45, 47 (4)
Bernard Lassus: 54, 55, 56 (2)
Fritz von Fürstenberg: 57
Bernd Krüger: 58 (2), 59
Krollpfeifer + Peukert: 60
Lisa Diedrich: 62 (3), 63 (3)
Kamel Louafi: 65 (3), 66 top centre, 66 central row (3), 66 bottom left and centre, 67 bottom left, 70 (2), 71
Robert Schäfer: 66 top left and right, 66 bottom right, 67 (3, except bottom left)
Dirk Meyerhöfer: 68/69
Frank Colder: 73, 74 (3), 75 left
Okra landschapsarchitecten: 75 right
Sarah Blee: 76, 78 (2)
Claudia Dulak: 78 top
Martin Sundström: 80
Bengt Isling: 83 (2)
Karres en Brands: 84 (10), 85 (10), 86 (10), 87 (10)
Claas Dreppenstedt: 89, 90, 91, 92, 93, 94, 95
Auböck/Kárász: 96, 97, 98 (2), 99

Dieses Buch ist 1999 als Zeitschrift bei Callwey unter der ISSN 0942-752-X erschienen.
This book exists also as a magazine at Callwey Publishers (ISSN 0942-752-X).

Translation from German into English: Almuth Seebohm, Judith Harrison, Bruce Roberts
Graphic Design: Sabine Hoffmann

A CIP catalogue record for this book is available from the Library of Congress, Washington D.C., USA.

Deutsche Bibliothek Cataloging-in-Publication Data

Stucco, stone and steel : new materials in open space design = Stuck, Stein und Stahl / Topos, European Landscape
Magazine (ed.). [Transl. from German into English: Almuth Seebohm ...]. - Basel ; Boston ; Berlin : Birkhäuser;
München : Callwey, 2001
ISBN 3-7643-6502-1

© 2001 Birkhäuser – Publishers for Architecture, P.O. Box 133, CH-4010 Basel, Switzerland
and Verlag Georg D. W. Callwey GmbH & Co. KG, Munich

Printed on acid-free paper produced from chlorine-free pulp. TCF ∞

Printed in Germany

ISBN 3-7643-6502-1

9 8 7 6 5 4 3 2 1